The Making of the Meiji Constitution

The Oligarchs and the Constitutional Development of Japan, 1868-1891

The Making of the Meiji Constitution

The Oligarchs and the Constitutional Development of Japan, 1868-1891

by
GEORGE M. BECKMANN
University of Kansas

Foreword by
HAROLD S. QUIGLEY
University of Minnesota (retired)

GREENWOOD PRESS, PUBLISHERS
WESTPORT, CONNECTICUT

Library of Congress Cataloging in Publication Data

Beckmann, George M
  The making of the Meiji Constitution.

  Reprint of the ed. published by the University of
Kansas Press, Lawrence; with new pref.
  Bibliography: p.
  1. Japan--Constitutional history. I. Japan.
Constitution. II. Title.
[JQ1611.B4 1975]   342'.52'029   72-7963
ISBN 0-8371-6553-9

© *1957 Committee on Social Science Studies*
University of Kansas Publications

Originally published in 1957 by University of Kansas Press,
Lawrence

Reprinted with the permission of George M. Beckmann

Reprinted in 1975 by Greenwood Press,
a division of Williamhouse-Regency Inc.

Library of Congress Catalog Card Number 72-7963

ISBN 0-8371-6553-9

Printed in the United States of America

Foreword

In the forty years between 1854 and 1894 Japan left the feudal and entered the modern age. She emerged from isolation and entered the international community. The Yamato dynasty was restored to dignity, if not to power. A system of government was established which has stood the test of time. The credit for these accomplishments must go to the men who perceived the necessity for political centralization, industrialization, and military power, and who worked loyally, if not selflessly, to bring to pass one of the most remarkable transformations which history records. Most of these men were seasoned samurai of four great clans—Satsuma, Choshu, Hizen and Tosa—men who were products and successful administrators of the feudal system but who saw the signs of the times—external and internal—and who were not bound by deference to institutions which they believed to be outmoded.

This scholarly monograph, based upon Japanese sources but taking account of pioneer work of Western students, adds importantly to our knowledge of the ideas and methods of the samurai leaders who operated as an unorganized oligarchy after the resignation of the last Tokugawa shogun and who manipulated or frustrated elements that demanded a liberal written constitution of 1889 for themselves and their successors until such time as democratic influences should grow strong enough to challenge *genro* prestige. Dr. Beckmann focuses upon the evolution of constitutional policy but he briefly interweaves political, economic, military, administrative, and other factors which affected that process. His main contribution, however, is his revelation of the varying views of the principal actors in the drama of the constitutional movement. Thereby he adds a greatly needed reality to the more impersonal treatments hitherto available. He also supplements valuably earlier accounts of the actual drafting of the Meiji constitution and of the influence upon it of Prussian and Austrian scholars. He appends ten documents, seven of which have not previously been published in English.

It is a pleasure and a privilege to commend this informative and interesting book to all who are concerned to understand the statesmanship of the Restoration period.

Harold S. Quigley

Preface to the Reprint Edition

In 1890 the government of Japan began to function according to the provisions of the Meiji Constitution. This fundamental law of the state, which was not replaced until the promulgation of the new constitution in 1947, was the culmination of the restoration of imperial rule in 1868 and several decades of political experimentation that followed. The new leaders of Japan, largely samurai from Choshu and Satsuma like Kido Koin, Okubo Toshimuchi, and Ito Hirobumi, had participated in the anti-Tokugawa movement and had come to realize that Japan could not be governed in the old manner. Faced with the challenge of the West, they saw the need for a new central government that could develop the nation's strength, reforming society where necessary. Utilizing imperial legitimacy, they cooperated in establishing an effective central administration in which they exercised political power in the name of the emperor. Faced with the question of whether to establish a representative assembly, they were attracted to German concepts on constitutionalism, which minimized the power of parliamentary bodies. When various discontented political factions began to agitate for representation in a national assembly, they were attracted to German concepts on constitutionalism, which minimized the power of parliamentary bodies. When various discontented political factions began to agitate for representation in a national assembly, the Satsuma-Choshu leaders, a dominant oligarchy, became determined to formulate a constitutional policy which would strengthen the state and provide a new legal justification for the imperial system which they controlled.

The major constitutional problem during the early Meiji period (1868-1890) was the establishment of a system of government that would maintain strong leadership under the emperor and at the same time include a representative assembly. The authoritarian bias of the oligarchs, their desire to catch up with the major Western powers, their intense commitment to national development, and their constant fear of factionalism in government caused them to reject British and French models of representative government and turn to the German model which maintained imperial supremacy. Increasing agitation by elements of the democratic movement forced the government in 1881 publicly to promise the establishment of a parliament. The oligarchs created a bicameral diet in the Meiji Constitution, but at the same time their guiding principle in drafting the constitution was the establishment of powerful civil and military executive agents under the emperor. They were determined to maintain strong executive leadership with the least possible sacrifice of power on their part.

In the final analysis, the Meiji Constitution provided a flexible foundation for subsequent political development. Under it, Japan moved gradually over four decades from oligarchical government toward responsible parliamentary government based on the shifting strength of political parties. However, the Meiji Constitution could not provide a sufficiently strong bulwark to maintain this line of development during the national crisis of the 1930's. In the end, the forces of ultranationalism and militarism were able to reverse this trend and dominate the political decision-making process.

The central problem of this monograph is to determine the origins of the constitutional policy of the oligarchs after 1868 and to trace its development until the promulgation of the Meiji Constitution in 1889.

Since the appearance of W. W. McLaren's pioneer work, *A Political History of Japan during the Meiji Era 1867-1912*, New York, 1916, Western specialists in history and political science have increasingly turned their attention to problems of politics and government during the Meiji period. Noteworthy among their works are the excellent analyses of the operation of Japanese government under the Meiji Constitution by Harold Quigley and Kenneth Colegrove and the histories of the

Meiji period by Sir George Sansom and E. Herbert Norman. Of the more recent works, Nobutaka Ike's *The Beginnings of Political Democracy in Japan,* Baltimore, 1950, is of special importance because of its treatment of the democratic movement in the Meiji period.

There is no account in Western languages of the development of the constitutional policy of the Japanese government in the early Meiji period, and the various constitutional histories by Japanese scholars are deficient in historical analysis and generally lacking in interpretation. The present study is an attempt to fill what is therefore a lacuna in the existing literature in the field of modern Japanese political history.

The author owes a substantial debt of thanks to several people who assisted in the preparation of this study. The author is most grateful to Drs. Thomas Smith and Arthur Wright, who made important suggestions. He is indebted to Dr. Nobutaka Ike, who proposed the topic and on whom the author relied heavily for bibliographical advice. He must also thank Dr. Francis Heller, his friend and colleague, for undertaking the onerous task of guiding the manuscript through the press, and he acknowledges the assistance of Okubo Genji of the Canadian Embassy in Tokyo in the translation of the appendices. Finally, the author wishes to thank the editors of *Hogaku kenkyu* (Journal of Law, Politics, and Sociology) at Keio University, Tokyo, for permission to include material published in Japan between 1953 and 1955.

Contents

Foreword v

Preface vii

I. The Meiji Revolution 1

II. The Abolition of Feudalism 12

III. The Oligarchy and Constitutionalism, 1871-1875 26

IV. The Oligarchy and the Democratic Movement, 1876-1881 ... 39

V. The Constitutional Debate, 1881-1885 53

VI. Drafting the Meiji Constitution, 1881-1889 69

VII. The Oligarchy and the Meiji Constitution 84

Bibliography 96

Appendices:
    I. Constitution Ordered to be Drafted by Kido Koin 100
    II. Okubo Toshimichi's Opinion on Constitutional Government 111
    III. Draft Constitution of the Genroin 120
    IV. Yamagata Aritomo's Opinion on Constitutional Government 126
    V. Ito Hirobumi's Opinion on Constitutional Government ... 131
    VI. Okuma Shigenobu's Opinion on Constitutional Government 136
    VII. Iwakura Tomomi's Opinion on Constitutional Government 143
    VIII. Imperial Rescript Promising the Establishment of Parliament 149
    IX. Preamble to the Constitution of the Empire of Japan ... 150
    X. Constitution of the Empire of Japan 151

Index 157

Chapter I
The Meiji Revolution

The coup d'etat of January 3, 1868, which abolished the Tokugawa Shogunate and established a new provisional central government in the name of the Emperor Meiji, opened a new era in the political and constitutional history of Japan. The restoration of imperial rule was the beginning of a series of political as well as economic and social reforms that ultimately transformed Japan from a decentralized nation of feudal *han* (kingdoms) into a highly centralized modern capitalist state.

The fundamental cause underlying this political revolution is a matter of great dispute among Japanese historians.[1] Their conflicting theses regarding the restoration can be explained in part by the extremely complicated economic and social changes that were occurring in the Tokugawa period and in part by ideological considerations.[2] However, there is common agreement on several important general characteristics. By mid-nineteenth century, Japanese society had suffered the impact of the penetration of capitalism on the village level. The feudal political system had deteriorated as economic power had shifted into the hands of the great merchants of Edo and Osaka and the rising merchant-landlord-industrialists (capitalists) of the towns and villages. The feudal ruling class of Japan was deeply in debt and faced impoverishment, but even harder hit were the lower-samurai (retainers), who were forced to accept drastic reductions in their annual stipends, and the peasantry, which was not only burdened by increased taxes but also, in many cases, at the mercy of the usury of

---

1. For an excellent brief summary of the major points in dispute between the two main divisions of Japanese left-wing historians, the "ronoha" and the "kozaha," see Toyama Shigeki, *Meiji ishin shi* (Tokyo, 1951), 11-17. The "kozaha" view of the controversy is summarized in Uchida Jokichi, *Nihon shihonshugi ronso;* the "ronoha," in Tsushima Tadayuki, *Nihon shihonshugi ronso shiron.*

2. This is particularly true of such "kozaha" historians as Hattori Shiso, Hirano Yoshitaro, and Toyama Shigeki, all of whom view the Meiji Restoration as the victory of the feudal-capitalist alliance in a class struggle with the peasantry and "urban proletariat."

1

THE MAKING OF THE MEIJI CONSTITUTION

the local capitalists. Almost every class or group in society was discontented and was taking measures to protect or improve its position. The *Bakufu* (Tokugawa military government) and many *daimyo* (feudal lords) strove to control the new capitalist forms of production and wealth; many lower-samurai and *ronin* (masterless samurai) became convinced that the destruction of the Tokugawa Shogunate was necessary to bring about fundamental changes in society; the peasantry resorted to open rebellion to enforce their demands for improved conditions; and finally, the rising merchant-landlord-industrialists bitterly resented the political and economic restrictions imposed upon their operations.

One important school of Japanese historians explains the Meiji Restoration and the subsequent development of Japan strictly in terms of these internal economic developments.[3] The validity of their thesis that internal conditions were leading to an inevitable political, economic, and social reconstruction of Japanese society cannot be denied; however, this argument tends to overlook a fact of critical importance. It was the impact of foreign political and economic pressures that hastened the organization of an active well-organized movement for political reform.[4] The warnings and teachings of such influential samurai scholars as Yoshida Shoin and Fujita Toko attest to the development of a feeling of nationalism; that many of their disciples were leaders of the anti-Tokugawa movement suggests the importance of their contribution to the creation of modern Japan.

These two factors, the disintegration of feudal society under the development of capitalism and the rise of a nationalism engendered by the fear of foreign domination, were the motivating forces behind the widespread demand for reform. The *daimyo,* their hereditary councillors, and elements within the *Bakufu*

---

3. The "kozaha" group refute or at least minimize the influence of foreign political and economic pressures in the development of the anti-Bakufu movement. See particularly Toyama, *op. cit.,* 45-52.

4. Ito Hirobumi, "Some Reminiscences of the Grant of the New Constitution," *Fifty Years of New Japan,* edited by Okuma Shigenobu (London, 1910), I, 122.

sought to strengthen the feudal system through the establishment of a loose federation of *han* under a union of the imperial court and the Tokugawa Shogunate. This program was especially attractive to the conservative political leaders of Satsuma and Choshu, for it promised an opportunity to extend their influence in a limited national administration. The *Bakufu* was also sympathetic to the idea of union as a convenient means of stabilizing the position of the Tokugawa family in face of increased anti-feudal agitation. Economic reform, to these same elements, meant nothing more than the consolidation and extension of their control over the new methods of production.[5]

A small group of samurai-intellectuals, who won the backing of the merchant-landlord-industrialists, saw the need for more drastic steps. As *han* bureaucrats, who had risen through ability, they had already begun to promote the adoption of western military science, and they utilized capital accumulated through monopolies to begin the manufacture of armaments. As a group, they urged a policy of modernization in order to strengthen the nation as well as their *han*. Politically they worked for the destruction of the Tokugawa Shogunate and the establishment of a more centralized national administration as a necessary preliminary to modernization on a national scale.

The movement to overthrow the Tokugawa Shogunate began in the 1850's as a series of secret and unconnected plots by samurai who were organized locally around some strong personality such as Yoshida Shoin and Fujita Toko. However, not until the 1860's was there a gradual integration of these groups into a national revolutionary movement. This was chiefly the accomplishment of discontented samurai and *ronin* who made their headquarters at Kyoto, where they won the support of many court nobles who had much to gain by the destruction of the Tokugawa Shogunate. While these groups plotted against the *Bakufu* in Kyoto, their confederates in the *han* worked to place the military and economic power of their *han* solidly behind the movement.

---
5. Toyama, *op. cit.*, 27-28, 34-37.

The Making of the Meiji Constitution

Utilizing the *Bakufu's* dilemma in foreign relations and playing upon the jealousy between Satsuma and Choshu, the samurai leaders of the modernization party, who gradually gained ascendency in their *han,* blocked the realization of the union plan and established the imperial court as a center of political power; moreover, the foreign bombardments of Kagoshima and Shimonoseki in 1863-1864 displayed dramatically and convincingly to Satsuma and Choshu that resistance to modernization was suicidal. Finally, after the military impotence of the *Bakufu* was disclosed in the Choshu campaign of 1866, Satsuma and Choshu openly entered into an anti-*Bakufu* alliance, which was soon joined by Tosa, Echizen, and Uwajima. This coalition of *han,* under the leadership of Saigo Takamori, Okubo Toshimichi, and Kido Koin, staged the coup d'etat of January 3, 1868. That the new central government was not a new Shogunate can be attributed to the balance of power within the coalition and to the fact that the victory of these samurai in the struggles for power within their *han* eliminated the possibility of some ambitious *daimyo* trying to seize power.

However, it is clear that the leaders of the successful anti-*Bakufu* coalition were not united on a policy of political reform. The lesser *han,* particularly Tosa, were gravely concerned about the possible usurpation of power by Satsuma and Choshu and the establishment of another Shogunate. To prevent this, Tosa had endeavored to work out a peaceful settlement between Satsuma and Choshu and the Tokugawa Shogunate through the restoration of imperial rule and the creation of a national federation of *han* based upon a representative assembly. According to the Tosa proposal, the *Shogun* would resign and participate in the government as head of the assembly and thus provide a powerful obstacle to the seizure of power by Satsuma and Choshu.[6] Tokugawa Keiki had complied with this plan as he saw in it a means of making a strategic withdrawal that would check the intention of Satsuma and Choshu to destroy the Shogunate by force. Keiki's

---

6. Osatake Takeki, *Nihon kensei shi taiko* (Tokyo, 1938), I, 74-75.

The Meiji Revolution

resignation in early November 1867 and the promulgation of an imperial edict summoning the representatives of forty *han* to Kyoto to approve the *Shogun's* formal surrender of power were the initial steps taken to implement the Tosa plan.[7]

The successful coup d'etat had prevented the realization of the Tosa plan; Saigo, Kido, and Okubo were suspicious of any compromise that would leave the Tokugawa power intact, and they showed no sympathy for a deliberative assembly, especially as it had become associated with an attempt to save the interests of the Tokugawa Shogunate.[8] However, the samurai leaders of Satsuma and Choshu were keenly aware that it was absolutely necessary to maintain the unity of the coalition against the resistance of the Tokugawa and their supporters to the demands of the new government. This resistance emphasized the importance of the fact that so long as the new central government had no military power of its own, political differences had to be avoided. It is no exaggeration to state that the political and constitutional history of Japan in the first three years of the Meiji era was largely conditioned by this emphasis upon political unity.

The formal organization of the provisional government established on January 3, 1868, was headed by the *Sosai* (Supreme Administrator) and included two councils and seven administrative departments. Prince Arisugawa was appointed *Sosai*, and his deputies *(Fukusosai)* were Iwakura Tomomi and Sanjo Sanetomi, court nobles friendly to Satsuma and Choshu. These appointments were calculated to emphasize the importance of the throne and the imperial court, whose power the military had usurped for so long. The councils were composed of court nobles, *daimyo*, and samurai, whose main function was to deliberate matters of importance and suggest measures to the *Sosai*, who was responsible for the administration. The administrative departments were headed by Princes-of-the-Blood or court nobles, who were at the

---

7. *Meiji shiyo,* Tokyo Imperial University Edition (Tokyo, 1933), I, 1.
8. Asai Kiyoshi, *Meiji rikken shiso ni okeru eikoku gikai seido no eikyo* (Tokyo, 1935), 225-227.

same time members of the councils. The whole organization was in reality a great council, the members of which not only formulated policy but administered it through their control of the various departments.

While the effective leadership of the samurai of the western *han* was able to prevent the establishment of another Shogunate, strong limitations upon their power had prevented the establishment of a powerful central government. The provisional government at Kyoto was merely an administration organized to perform the functions formerly exercised by the *Bakufu*. No immediate attempts were made to interfere with the existing *han* regimes; in fact, the *daimyo* were given preëminent positions in the government in recognition of their support. The appointment of *daimyo* and court nobles to high offices was in reality a skillful maneuver by the samurai leaders to maintain the continued support of the *han* and to utilize the prestige of the imperial court as a powerful sanction for their program. The real power remained in the hands of such revolutionary samurai as Kido, Saigo, Okubo, Goto Shojiro, and Okuma Shigenobu, who held positions strategically located within the office of the *Sosai* and in the administrative departments which enabled them to formulate and guide policy.[9] An unofficial oligarchy was beginning to emerge.

The most pressing problem that faced the new government was to crush Tokugawa resistance which broke out against the demand that the Tokugawa family surrender its vast lands. In order to gain the military and political coöperation necessary to bring the civil war to a successful conclusion, the samurai leaders of Satsuma and Choshu were forced to meet the demands of Tosa for an assembly that would broaden the basis of administration. Thus, in January, the government accepted the proposal of Goto and Fukuoka Kotei for the creation of a bicameral assembly (*Gijisho*) in which all the *han* would be represented by *daimyo*

---

9. Fujii Jintaro and Moriya Hidesuke, *Sogo nihon shi taikei: Meiji jidai shi* (Tokyo, 1940), 239-240. *Meiji shiyo*, I, 6.

and samurai.[10] When the government was reorganized in early February, it included an upper house of court nobles and *daimyo* and a lower house composed of samurai representatives from all the *han,* apportioned on the basis of three representatives for the large *han,* two for the intermediate, and one for the small, as well as an unspecified number of appointed representatives.[11] These bodies were only called into session several times, and lacking the coöperation of the oligarchs, their deliberations were a failure.[12]

Shortly thereafter, on February 26, the government issued an imperial rescript calling for the assistance of the whole nation against the forces of the ex-*Shogun;* however, this appeal was based upon a perfunctory declaration of the Emperor's absolute authority.[13] The leaders of the government soon realized that it was necessary to announce a policy that would have greater popular appeal. Of particular importance were the financial factors that caused the samurai in power to adopt a more compromising attitude. To finance the civil war, the provisional government, whose income was limited to the meager revenues of the imperial lands, had issued unbacked paper currency amounting to seventy-two per cent of the budget; moreover, the bulk of the remainder of the budget was provided by loans from the great urban merchants. These factors help to explain the famous *Charter Oath,* which was issued in April by the government in the name of the Emperor. The circumstances surrounding its promulgation give the impression that the oath was nothing more than a general statement of policy consciously designed to unite the whole nation behind the efforts of its leaders.[14] As for its political promises, the oath was a concession by means of which the leaders of the government sought to allay dissatisfaction while they devoted themselves to immediate problems.

---

10. Ishin Shiryo Hensan Jimukyoku, *Ishin shi* (Tokyo, 1939-1941), V, 519-521.
11. *Meiji shiyo,* I, 25.
12. *Ishin shi,* V, 222.
13. W. W. McLaren, ed., "Japanese Government Documents," *Transactions of the Asiatic Society of Japan,* 42 (May 1914), 6-7.
14. Fujii and Moriya, *op. cit.,* 13-16.

THE MAKING OF THE MEIJI CONSTITUTION

Shortly after the promulgation of the *Charter Oath,* Fukuoka again memorialized the government to convoke an assembly in accordance with the intention of the oath.[15] The government took this opportunity to order Fukuoka and Soejima Taneomi to draw up a plan for the general reorganization of the government. After several conferences in which Fukuoka and Soejima presented various draft proposals, the government promulgated the *Seitaisho* on June 17, 1868, and it was officially announced that the government was being reorganized with a view to the fulfilment of the *Charter Oath.*

The reorganization of the government under the *Seitaisho*[16] clearly demonstrates the tendency for the samurai leaders of Satsuma and Choshu to consolidate their positions of power; moreover, these leaders made a general claim for the supreme authority of the central government in the *Seitaisho,* which stated that the *han* were subordinate to the new central administration. On the other hand, since the samurai were still aware of the absolute necessity of a policy of tact and compromise, they continued to bestow high offices on a few important *daimyo,* and left all the *daimyo* in their hereditary positions as *han* rulers.

The actual operation of the new system of government resulted in the concentration of power in the upper house *(jokyoku)* of the assembly *(Giseikan);* moreover, the centralization of political authority was carried a step further, since the upper house was effectively controlled by its samurai members. These samurai leaders also directed departmental administration through the appointment of capable samurai compatriots to the office of deputy minister or to some other key office within each department. Since the ministers were court nobles or *daimyo* who were usually figureheads, these appointees were able to manage the actual workings of the administrative system. Thus, for all practical purposes, the samurai leaders were able to dominate the govern-

---

15. Miyakoshi Shinichiro, ed., *Nihon kensei kiso shiryo* (Tokyo, 1939), 51.
16. *Ibid.,* 38-50. See also R. A. Wilson, "The Seitaisho: A Constitutional Experiment" in "Problems of Political Power in Modern Japan, A Symposium," *The Far Eastern Quarterly,* XI (1952), 297-304.

ment through the concentration of political power in the upper house and through their control of the administrative departments.

The lower house (*kakyoku*)[17] of the bicameral assembly, on the other hand, was nothing more than an advisory body created to satisfy the demands for representation in the government put forward by the leaders of the lesser *han*. Its functions were directed by the upper house and were confined to the mere discussion of matters pertaining to national affairs as well as the settlement of disputes between the *han*. The lower house met several times, but the limited nature of its power and the inexperience of its members resulted in its failure as a deliberative body. It was composed largely of samurai who had little experience in politics and whose interests were more local than national. Moreover, it was given no encouragement by the samurai leaders of Satsuma and Choshu, who desired a strong government unhampered by legislative limitations.[18] As a result, the meetings of the lower house were abandoned in the autumn of 1868.

The assembly idea, however, persisted among the leaders of the lesser *han*,[19] and the subsequent establishment of the *Kogisho* in April 1869 and the *Shugiin* in August 1869 were the result of their continued demands for representation. That the oligarchs gave in to these demands in no way implied a desire to experiment with representative government. The extremely limited functions and powers of the *Kogisho* and *Shugiin* contradict this contention. These concessions were largely an appeasement policy designed to maintain political harmony, for, once the Tokugawa resistance was suppressed, the samurai leaders of Satsuma and Choshu became intent upon the abolition of the *han* in order to establish the absolute supremacy of the central government. Leaders like Kido, Okubo, and Iwakura had come to realize that the abolition of the *han* was essential for the modernization of Japan; moreover, the creation of a national army was necessary to end the government's

---

17. This name was soon changed to *koshi taisakusho*.
18. Miyakoshi, *Nihon kensei kiso shiryo*, 10.
19. Osatake Takeki, *Ishin zengo ni okeru rikken shiso* (Tokyo, 1929), II, 427-429.

dependence upon the military support of the *han*. The well-known history of these reforms from the March 1869 memorial of the four great *han* to the formal abolition of all the *han* in 1871 is an indication of the statesmanship of these oligarchs in persuading the powerful western *han* to accept their program. That they proceeded slowly and cautiously reflects their great concern to maintain a maximum of political unity during these turbulent years.

The failure of the assemblies to become an integral part of the government can be explained in large part by the lack of encouragement given to them by the samurai leaders of Satsuma and Choshu, who were intent upon the establishment of an efficient authoritarian regime. These samurai, confronted by considerations of national defense as well as economic and social problems, desired a government which would be capable of implementing their program to strengthen Japan through modernization. That they found it expedient to turn to the examples of the absolutist bureaucratic governments of the *han* and Prussia[20] was only natural; moreover, leaders like Okubo tended to regard the assemblies as useless organs of government or as mechanisms which their political opponents could use advantageously. However, until the abolition of the *han* in 1871, these assemblies did help to maintain the stability of the government in face of the demands of the lesser *han*. After the abolition of the *han*, the assemblies were of no appreciable use to the government and were replaced by organs that were more consistent with the operations of an authoritarian regime.

On the other hand, it is clear that the demand for a representative assembly had no mass basis in the early years of the Meiji era. The tradition of authoritarian government based upon a rigid caste and family system had prevented the development of equalitarian ideals and a sense of individual rights among the common people. Japanese legal institutions were not based on correlations of rights and duties, and even Japanese feudalism lacked the bi-

---

20. Even in these early years of the Meiji era there were numerous references to the government of Prussia and Bismarck in the papers of Okubo and Iwakura.

lateral elements that characterized it in the West. Thus there existed no mass demand that the government be responsible to public opinion. The demands for a national assembly actually represented the interests of the lesser *han,* particularly Tosa, which feared the domination of Satsuma and Choshu; however, the assemblies were far too limited in power to prevent the development of an oligarchy of strong-willed samurai and court nobles.

Chapter II
The Abolition of Feudalism

The *han* had remained intact after the Meiji Restoration because the objective of the coalition of the western *han* had been limited to the destruction of the Tokugawa Shogunate. Although the movement against the Shogunate had been led by revolutionary samurai, who were soon intent upon the abolition of the *han* as a necessary preliminary to the establishment of a strong centralized state, its success had depended upon the military support of the western *han*, which merely desired the creation of a limited central government to replace the *Bakufu*. The samurai who became the leaders of the new central government realized that they were dependent upon the continued support of the *han*; consequently, they made no immediate attempts to interfere with the existing *han* regimes. They were equally aware, however, that the success of their intention to establish a strong central government necessitated the abolition of the *han* but, because of the weakness of the central government, they moved slowly to ensure domestic peace and to prevent the coalition of loyal *han* from dissolving.

The June 1868 reorganization of the administration of the Tokugawa lands was the starting point in the creation of a centralized state. The central government, which had confiscated these lands during the civil war, converted them into prefectures (*ken*) and at the same time organized the cities of Osaka, Kyoto, and Tokyo as special administrative districts called *fu*. Governors who were responsible to the central government were appointed to supervise the administration of the *fu* and *ken*. That samurai of outstanding ability, such as Ito Hirobumi and Yuri Kimmasa, were appointed governors attests to the importance the leaders of the central government attached to these posts.[1] Thus, in an area comprising one-fourth of the entire country, the central govern-

---
1. McLaren, *Japanese Government Documents*, 22; Fujii and Moriya, *Sogo nihon shi taikei*, 271-272.

The Abolition of Feudalism

ment managed to establish local governments that were completely under its control. However, the remainder of the country was divided among the *han*, which continued to be virtually independent of the central government.

In the *Seitaisho*, the samurai leaders of Satsuma and Choshu began to take positive measures regarding the *han*. They put forward the doctrine that the supreme power and authority of Japan rested in the *Dajokan*, but they did not attempt to overturn the *han* administrations. Instead, they undertook a policy designed to standardize *han* offices in order to facilitate business and relations between the central government and the *han*. In July 1868, the office of *Kokunin*, later changed to *Koginin*, was established in each *han* to be filled by a *daimyo* appointee who would act as an intermediary between the central government and the *han*.[2] In December of the same year, the offices of *Shissei* and *Sansei* were added to create an enlarged uniform organization of government in all the *han;* these officials were appointed by the *daimyo* but, like the *Koginin*, they were subject to imperial authority.[3] The *han* were also urged to convoke assemblies modeled on the *Kogisho*.[4]

While these developments represented significant progress in the standardization of the *han* governments, the leaders of the central government remained intent upon their primary purpose, the abolition of the *han*. Kido Koin, particularly, was convinced of the need to centralize government power and functions under the supreme authority of the Emperor. Although the government had received many memorials urging the conversion of the *han* into *ken* by an imperial order, Kido did not think it wise to attempt an outright confiscation because the success of such a venture would ultimately depend upon the attitude of the *daimyo* and their conservative councillors. Instead, Kido and Okubo persuaded the *daimyo* of Choshu and Satsuma to return the title to their

---

2. McLaren, *Japanese Government Documents*, 25-26.
3. *Ibid.*, 26-27.
4. *Ibid.*, 27; Miyakoshi, *Nihon kensei kiso shiryo*, 61-62.

lands to the Emperor voluntarily. Finally, the consent of Tosa and Hizen was secured through the joint efforts of Okubo, Itagaki, and Hirosawa Sanetomi.[5]

The efforts of Kido, Okubo, Itagaki, and Hirosawa culminated in the March 5, 1869, memorial, signed by the *daimyo* of Choshu, Satsuma, Tosa, and Hizen, in which these four lords recognized the supremacy of the central government and offered their lands to the Emperor. This document, thought to have been written by Kido, is evidence of the nationalistic outlook of the samurai leaders of the central government.[6] It states: "There must be one central authority which must be preserved intact"; and adds: "All laws, decrees, military regulations, extending even to military dress and accoutrement [will] be issued by the central government, so that all matters of state [will] be decided by one and the same authority."[7]

On March 6, the day following the submission of the memorial, the central government approved the transfer of the land titles; however, a satisfactory means of implementing the memorial had to be found. The question was submitted to a special council of *daimyo,* court nobles, and government officials, which was about to convene in Tokyo as the upper house of the assembly.[8] On the whole, the council was divided between two opinions. The court nobles, the lesser *daimyo,* and a group of samurai officials led by Ito Hirobumi advocated the abolition of the *han* and the immediate extension of the prefecture system. Kido, Okubo, and their followers agreed to this in principle, but they felt that the government was not yet strong enough to carry out such an action. Kido and Okubo thought that for the time being it would be better to maintain the *han* as they were with the *daimyo* and their retainers as imperial officials responsible for the *han* administration.[9] This cautious stand by Kido and Okubo, based upon a

---

5. Fujii and Moriya, *Sogo nihon shi taikei,* 309-310.
6. The full text is translated in McLaren, *Japanese Government Documents,* 29-32.
7. *Ibid.,* 32.
8. Fujii and Moriya, *Sogo nihon shi taikei,* 312.
9. *Ibid.,* 312, 316.

THE ABOLITION OF FEUDALISM

realistic appraisal of the political situation, can also be explained in part by the attitude of the *daimyo* of the four great *han*. Evidence indicates that these *daimyo* had proposed the return of their lands only as a formal gesture of recognition of the supremacy of the central government and that they expected only a nominal change in the administration of their *han*.[10]

In an imperial decree issued on July 25, 1869, the central government announced the policy it intended to follow. The surrender of land by the four great *han* was officially accepted and the remainder of the *han* were ordered to follow suit. The old orders of nobility were abolished, with the court nobles and *daimyo* becoming *kazoku,* a newly created nominal designation of nobility. At the same time, the *daimyo* were appointed as governors of their *han* with an annual allowance of one-tenth of their former revenues. Their samurai were given a fixed income corresponding to a variant fraction of their former stipends. The central government, on the other hand, was recognized as the supreme authority in the country, but more important, the financial position of the government was improved by securing complete control of the power to tax.[11]

Throughout 1869 and 1870, an important debate regarding the status of the *han* commanded the attention of the leaders of the government. Kido and Okubo soon realized that it was necessary to extend the prefecture system to all the *han*. On April 20, 1870, they met in secret with Inouye Kaoru, Yamagata Aritomo, Iwakura, and Sanjo to work out their plans. All agreed that the 1869 compromise solution, which had been adopted as a temporary measure, was highly unsatisfactory for a number of reasons. It was impossible for the central government to direct the administration of the *han* effectively so long as the ex-*daimyo* and their

---

10. For a discussion of the intentions of the *daimyo*, see *ibid.*, 314-315. It is interesting to note that the most conservative stand within the government on this question was taken by the *Kogisho*, which was split between two opinions: one, to let the *han* remain as they were, and the other, that of Kido and Okubo, which was merely a change in form. *Ibid.*, 317-318.

11. McLaren, *Japanese Government Documents,* 32; Fujii and Moriya, *Sogo nihon shi taikei,* 313-314.

retainers remained as officials; moreover, the old feudal loyalties persisted, and the people acted as if still living under the feudal system. There was also a conspicuous tendency for the *han* to lag behind the prefectures in the enactment of legislation, and in some cases the greater *han* purposely opposed reforms ordered by the central government.[12] On the other hand, many of the smaller *han*, unable to maintain a stable financial position, either petitioned the government for economic relief or became prefectures with their ex-*daimyo* and samurai resigning administrative control for a guarantee of their incomes.[13]

A group led by Soejima Taneomi, a Hizen samurai, opposed this action on the ground that it might precipitate a conflict with the *han* and thereby risk all that had been accomplished so far.[14] This lack of unanimity was a concern to Kido and Okubo, but a more important factor made them hesitate to take action. The ex-*daimyo* of Satsuma and Choshu, Shimazu and Mori, had seemingly withdrawn their support from the government and refused to participate in its deliberations; moreover, Saigo Takamori, at odds with Okubo over the fact that Satsuma had not a greater role in the government, had left Tokyo and returned to Kagoshima.[15]

In November 1870, Kido and Okubo worked out a plan to regain the coöperation of Saigo, Shimazu, and Mori prior to the abolition of the *han*. Okubo sent Saigo Tsugumichi to Satsuma to persuade his brother to rejoin the government. Saigo Takamori agreed and suggested that either Sanjo or Iwakura, acting as imperial messengers, undertake to persuade Mori and Shimazu to do the same. In February 1871, following this advice, the government sent Iwakura together with Kido and Okubo. Iwakura and Okubo proceeded to Satsuma under the pretext of delivering imperial swords as gifts for the shrine of Shimazu Nariakira. There they conferred with Shimazu Hisamitsu and Saigo and won their

---
12. Fujii and Moriya, *Sogo nihon shi taikei*, 261-262.
13. *Ibid.*, 319-320.
14. *Ibid.*, 327.
15. *Ibid.*, 259-260.

The Abolition of Feudalism

consent to return to Tokyo and participate in the government. In the meantime, Kido had gone to Choshu to confer with Mori. On February 26, he was joined by Iwakura, Okubo, and Saigo; they persuaded Mori to comply with the wishes of the government. Okubo, Saigo, and Kido then turned their attention to Tosa and met at Kochi with Itagaki Taisuke and Fukuoka Kotei, who agreed to join the government provided they were given positions of responsibility.[16]

By this series of events, the central government was reunited on the basis of a coalition of the samurai leaders of Satsuma, Choshu, and Tosa, who began to plan the abolition of the *han*. In April 1871, they organized an armed force of ten thousand men based upon requisitions from Satsuma, Choshu, and Tosa. Iwakura visited the former Tokugawa *han* of Owari and Hikone to secure their allegiance and coöperation.[17] By August, the stage was set for the abolition of the *han*. Fortified by new military strength and armed with the consent of the ex-*daimyo* of Satsuma, Choshu, Tosa, and Hizen, the oligarchs issued an imperial decree which stated simply: "The *han* are abolished, and prefectures are established in their places."[18] The ex-*daimyo* were removed from their posts as governors, and the central government began an immediate reorganization of the system of local government.

The position of Kido, Okubo, Saigo, and Itagaki as influential samurai in their *han* goes a long way in explaining the consent of Satsuma, Choshu, and Tosa to the abolition of the *han*. However, there were other factors that tended to make the objective of the central government easier to accomplish. Since the restoration, the great *han* had been fearful of another civil war that might result from an attempt by any one of them to seize power. More important was the fact that many younger samurai within these *han* wanted a broad national government in which they could find employment for their talents. These *han* were also increasingly

---

16. *Ibid.*, 327, 329-330.
17. *Ibid.*, 330-331. For the contributions of each *han* to the imperial army, see *Japan Weekly Mail* (Yokohama), June 6, 1872, 3.
18. The entire text is translated in McLaren, *Japanese Government Documents*, 32-33.

THE MAKING OF THE MEIJI CONSTITUTION

guided by a feeling of national prestige that had developed from a sense of loyalty to the Emperor and a desire to meet the foreign powers on terms of equality.[19] Finally, all the *han* had specific economic advantages to gain by adhering to the policy of the central government. In the case of the smaller *han*, their financial distress made them active supporters of the extension of the prefecture system so long as the incomes of their ex-*daimyo* and samurai were guaranteed. Economic considerations were also important to the ex-*daimyo* of the greater *han*, who saw advantages to be gained in coming to terms with the central government. As early as 1869, the ex-*daimyo* governors had been granted one-tenth of their former revenues and at the same time they were relieved of the expenses of administration and samurai stipends. Later, when their annual income payments were commuted into bonds issued by the government, which also assumed much of the ex-*daimyo* indebtedness, they used their capitalized pensions to buy large tracts of former common-land and to enter business as large-scale investors.[20] Thus, while the great ex-*daimyo* lost their political power—which in many cases had existed in name only—their financial position distinctly improved so that many of them became great landlords or industrial-banking capitalists. On the other hand, by this generous settlement, the oligarchs maintained the allegiance of the great lords to the central government.[21]

The samurai, in general, did not fare so well. Their stipends, which had been assumed by the government in 1869, were calculated at rates rising from 10 percent of their previous incomes. This settlement was inadequate for most samurai, who were finding it difficult to adjust their lives to the government's program of modernization; moreover, in the following years, additional reforms destroyed their feudal rights and privileges, while the establishment of national conscription broke their monopoly of

---

19. Sir George B. Sansom, *The Western World and Japan* (New York, 1950), 324.
20. For a list of the capitalized pensions of the great *daimyo*, see E. H. Norman, "Feudal Background of Japanese Politics," Ninth Conference of the Institute of Pacific Relations, Secretariat Paper No. 9 (New York, 1945), 50.
21. E. H. Norman, *Japan's Emergence as a Modern State* (New York, 1940), 99-100, 116n.

The Abolition of Feudalism

military service. Finally, the government, pressed by financial difficulties, was forced to repudiate the pension scheme of 1869, which amounted to 25 percent of its annual budget, and in December 1873, a voluntary system of pension commutation was announced to relieve the financial distress of the government and to encourage samurai, paid off in bonds and cash, to use their capital to enter business and buy land.[22] When this voluntary plan failed, the government, in 1876, put into operation a compulsory commutation scheme.[23] The advantages for the government were twofold. Its annual payments to the samurai were halved and a claim without term was reduced to a twenty-year lump-sum obligation. For thousands of samurai, however, the commutation settlement did not provide sufficient income for the support of their families. All these developments tended to make the samurai resentful of the modernization program of the government, and the samurai class came to provide the foundation of a militant conservative reaction that culminated in the Satsuma Rebellion of 1877.

After the abolition of the *han* in August 1871, the central government began an immediate reorganization of the system of local administration. The *han* were all converted into prefectures[24] and, by amalgamation, the number of prefectures was reduced from 302 to seventy-two.[25] Prefectural administration was headed by a governor who was responsible to the central government for the execution of policy.[26] The prefectures were divided into districts *(gun)*, cities *(ku)*, towns *(machi)*, and villages *(mura)*, the

---

22. McLaren, *Japanese Government Documents*, 558-562.
23. *Ibid.*, 562-566. For a chart of the rates of interest and the time allowance for maturity of the bonds issued by the government as payment to the samurai, see Norman, *Japan's Emergence*, 95.
24. For a table of the plan of conversion, see *Japan Weekly Mail*, April 6, 1872, 180-183.
25. McLaren, *Japanese Government Documents*, 251. By 1890, the number of prefectures was reduced to forty-five.
26. *Ibid.*, 277-285, 285-286. In 1873, the Department of Home Affairs was reestablished, and in 1874, it was given control over the entire local government system. This ministry, headed by Okubo, helped to account for the peculiarly centralized nature of the Japanese government. Every matter of importance concerning a locality had to be brought before the Department of Home Affairs by the local authorities, and the action to be taken virtually declared by the central government. *Ibid.*, 36-41.

officials of which were appointed by the prefectural governor and responsible to him for the local administration.[27] Thus, by a careful reorganization of local government under a highly centralized bureaucracy, the oligarchs extended and consolidated their control over the whole nation.

The destruction of the feudal system also paved the way for important changes in the organization of the central government. Conscious of the new administrative responsibilities that the abolition of the *han* would entail, the samurai leaders formed, in July 1871, a committee to draft a plan for the reorganization of the central government. This committee, headed by Kido, Saigo, and Okubo and including Itagaki, Goto, Okuma, Ito, and Inouye, adopted a draft proposal submitted by Goto and Eto Shimpei, a Hizen samurai, which was based upon a modified version of the "separation-of-powers" principle.[28] The *Dajokan* was divided into three boards: the Central Board *(Seiin)*, an executive body presided over by the *Dajodaijin*, the Right Board *(Uin)*, which included only the heads of the administrative departments, and the Left Board *(Sain)*, a legislative branch that replaced the *Shugiin*.[29]

The *Seiin*, as the supreme organ of the government, was entrusted with the supervision of the affairs of state. It discussed policy and rendered decisions in the presence of the Emperor on the most important matters of state. Its presiding officer was the *Dajodaijin*, and its members included the *Dainagon*[30] and an undetermined number of Councillors *(Sangi)*, an office monopolized by the samurai leaders, who, on the basis of their increased prestige and power, had abolished those high-ranking positions formerly held by court nobles and *daimyo*. At first, at the suggestion of Okubo, only Kido and Saigo were appointed to the office of *Sangi*. However, soon thereafter, Itagaki and Okuma were made Councillors in recognition of the support of Tosa and Hizen and as a

---

27. *Ibid.*, 270-271.
28. Osatake, *Nihon kensei shi taiko*, I, 284-285; Fujii and Moriya, *Sogo nihon shi taikei*, 440-441.
29. McLaren, *Japanese Government Documents*, 34-35.
30. This office was subsequently abolished and replaced by the Minister of the Right *(Udaijin)* and the Minister of the Left *(Sadaijin)*.

The Abolition of Feudalism

symbol of the theoretical equality of Satsuma, Choshu, Tosa, and Hizen.[31]

The *Uin,* whose members included the ministers of departments and deputy ministers, drafted departmental ordinances and regulations, handled the collective business of the departments, and discussed problems of administration.[32] In theory, the *Uin* was a separate body in the *Dajokan,* but in practice it became a mere adjunct of the *Seiin,* since there was a tendency for the court nobles and the ex-*daimyo* to be replaced as ministers of departments and deputy ministers by samurai who were concurrently Councillors of the *Seiin.* Thus, by a system of dual control, the samurai were able to maintain effective supervision over both the formation of policy and its administration.[33] At the same time, the government administrative structure, which was rapidly being expanded to handle the government's new responsibilities, was being permeated by personnel that was largely recruited from the samurai class.[34]

The legislative functions of the government were in theory vested in the *Sain,* whose members were appointed by the Emperor to represent public opinion but, because of strict limitations upon its powers and functions, the *Sain* was nothing more than a legislative advisory body under the complete control of the *Seiin.* All the measures that it considered were proposed by the *Seiin,* which had the power to appoint and dismiss *Sain* members in

---

31. Fujii and Moriya, *Sogo nihon shi taikei,* 331-332. Later, when the number of Councillors was increased, the unity of leadership in the government was maintained by the creation of an inner council called the *Naikaku Kaigi.*
32. There were numerous changes in the number of departments during these years. The following departments were included in the administration by the 1871 reorganization: Foreign Affairs, Finance, War, Public Works, Imperial Household, Education, Shinto, and Justice. The following changes occurred in the next few years: The Department of Shinto, abolished in April 1872, was replaced by the Department of Religion, which in November 1872 merged with the Department of Education; the Department of War was replaced by the Department of the Army and the Department of the Navy in February 1872; in November 1873, the Department of Home Affairs was re-established, having been formerly merged with the Department of Finance. McLaren, *Japanese Government Documents,* 35-36; Fujii and Moriya, *Sogo nihon shi taikei,* 441-445.
33. Fujii and Moriya, *Sogo nihon shi taikei,* 440-441.
34. Norman, *Japan's Emergence,* 83.

the name of the Emperor.[35] That this body was created at all can only be explained by the desire of the samurai oligarchy to have in existence an assembly which they could use to counter complaints against the concentration of power in their hands.

With their position of leadership made more secure by the abolition of the *han* and the reorganization of the central government, the oligarchs undertook a series of social, military, and economic reforms to mold Japan into a strong nation capable of meeting the foreign powers on terms of equality.[36] Soon after the Meiji Restoration, they had instituted reforms to put an end to feudal customs and practices that tended to obstruct the progress of modernization. One of the great obstacles was the rigid feudal caste system based upon occupation; by 1872 this system was replaced by a new class structure based upon legal equality. However, differences remained in social attitudes based upon tradition; moreover, as Japan developed into a modern bureaucratic state, new criteria of social position were established. The traditional feeling of social hierarchy remained strong, and social position tended to correspond to official position and to a lesser extent to wealth. Thus although the feudal class barriers were abolished, there was no strong equalitarian trend in the early Meiji period.[37]

The government also carried out important military reforms. Since the Meiji Restoration, it had been the desire of the oligarchs to concentrate military power in the central government in order to guarantee political stability.[38] After the abolition of the *han* in 1871 and the disestablishment of the samurai as a distinct class,

---

35. For the regulations of the *Sain*, see Miyakoshi, *Nihon kensei kiso shiryo*, I, 254-257.

36. This objective was extremely important to leaders like Okubo and Kido, who felt that rapid modernization required the effective direction of an authoritarian government. In the imperial rescript announcing the abolition of the *han*, the Emperor spoke for them: "We are of the opinion that in a time of radical reform like the present, if We desire by its means to give protection and tranquillity to the people at home, and abroad to maintain equality with foreign nations, words must be made in reality what they claim to signify, and the government of the country must center in a single authority." McLaren, *Japanese Government Documents*, 32-33.

37. Sansom, *The Western World and Japan*, 351.

38. E. H. Norman, *Soldier and Peasant in Japan: The Origins of Conscription* (New York, 1943), 42. For a summary of the military policy of the central government in these years, see Okuma, *Fifty Years of New Japan*, 201-202.

the oligarchs began to take steps towards the adoption of a national conscription system. In February 1872, the War Department was divided into the Department of the Army and the Department of the Navy, and in the following year, the government proclaimed military conscription based upon the Prussian system.[39] In the next few years, the army developed along Prussian lines and soon became a bulwark of the oligarchs' power. It successfully defended the government against its conservative opponents and, in the hands of the oligarchs, became a powerful political instrument.

The rapid industrialization of the country was perhaps the primary economic objective of the oligarchs,[40] for this goal was conceived of not only as a means of creating a strong Japan but also as a solution to various economic problems. The unfavorable foreign-trade balance and the devastating effect of imported manufactured goods on domestic handicraft production resulted in economic paternalism on the part of the government. Private capital was too weak to undertake an industrial program of the magnitude contemplated by the oligarchs, and the capital that was available was largely in the hands of the former guild merchants, who lacked the capacity to undertake a program of industrialization.[41] Thus the government itself developed heavy industry and communications and led the way in the expansion of consumer industries by establishing model factories, supplying technical assistance, and granting generous loans and subsidies to a few favored individuals who gradually emerged as a financial-industrial oligarchy, closely connected with the leaders of the government.[42]

The creation of a national army and the beginnings of industrialization placed a great strain upon the financial resources

---

39. For a description of the conscription system, see *Japan Weekly Mail*, March 1, 1873, 137-140.
40. For a convenient summary of Japan's industrialization in this period, see Norman, *Japan's Emergence*, 104-135.
41. *Ibid.*, 82.
42. *Ibid.*, 133.

of the government, and since Japan was predominantly agricultural and lacked tariff autonomy under the "unequal treaties," the land tax was made the major source of revenue. The land tax was modernized by a series of land laws passed in 1872 and 1873 in order to establish a budget system in which there were no unexpected revenue fluctuations resulting from annual variations in the size of the harvest. An official land survey was begun in January 1872, and title deeds to the land were issued to the peasants who were recognized as proprietors. In March, restrictions upon the alienation of land were removed, thereby facilitating the recognition of the claims of local landlords who, under the Tokugawa regime, had been acquiring land by mortgage and forced sale. The land-tax system was reorganized by an 1873 law which stipulated that the land tax was to be paid in money by the holder of the title deed at the rate of 3 percent of the assessed value of the land.[43]

These developments consolidated the position of the landlords, who tended to become the political foundation of the central government's power in the rural areas. The government legalized their property claims and, by guaranteeing a part of the pre-restoration debts of the military class to these landlord-usurers, it supplied them with additional funds for investment in industry or land.[44]

On the other hand, the peasant continued to suffer from the penetration of capitalism into the rural economy. The burden of the heavy land tax (amounting to 30-40 percent of the crop) fell on farmers whose holdings were rarely sufficient to produce more than a bare subsistence. As a result, the concentration of land ownership and tenancy continued to increase.[45] The peasants, bitterly disappointed by the agrarian settlement of the Meiji Restoration and resentful of such innovations as conscription, re-

---

43. *Ibid.*, 137-142; J. H. Gubbins, *The Making of Modern Japan* (London, 1912), 99-101. For a general survey of agricultural development, see Norman, *Japan's Emergence*, 70-80, 136-167.
44. Norman, *Japan's Emergence*, 98.
45. *Ibid.*, 143-148.

THE ABOLITION OF FEUDALISM

volted sporadically against their oppressors. These peasant revolts, which reached a peak in 1873, were suppressed by the iron hand of the government, which refused to alter the land settlement.[46] However, the discontent of the peasants could not be eradicated, and they remained a potential source of opposition to the ruling groups of Japan.[47]

The abolition of the *han* was the decisive step on the road to centralization of political power and modernization of the country. The government reorganization of September 1871 strengthened the supremacy of the Satsuma-Choshu oligarchs, while the *daimyo* pension-compensation program, the land legislation of 1872-1873, and the industrialization policies of the government won the general support of the former *daimyo*, the landlords, and the emerging financial-industrial combines, all of which profited by the process of change.

However, in the confusion and upset caused by these important changes, several groups in society became dissatisfied and even resentful. Many local landlords, who were also small industrialists, complained of the fiscal policies of the government, which placed the heaviest tax burden upon the land, and they resented the economic favoritism shown to a few favored urban industrialists. The peasantry, on the whole, were discontented, while wage earners were hit hard by inflation. It was these groups that the leaders of the lesser *han* later organized into a formidable political opposition to the government. Finally, and perhaps of the greatest imminent danger to the oligarchs, were the samurai, who were more likely than the other groups to resort to force to voice their discontent.

---

46. *Ibid.*, 72-73. However, for a time, the tax rate was reduced to 2½ percent.
47. For a discussion of the factors involved in the rise of peasant discontent, see Nobutaka Ike, *The Beginnings of Political Democracy in Japan* (Baltimore, 1950), 77-82.

Chapter III
The Oligarchy and Constitutionalism, 1871-1875

The question of a constitution emerged as an important issue in the early years of the Meiji era. The oligarchs, whose attention was devoted to the solution of such practical problems as industrialization and the development of military power, were determined to create a national sovereign state, and they came to feel that the best road to national reconstruction lay in strengthening the institutions of imperial government. The Emperor would be the ultimate authority for reform. Their political program grew out of the practical requirements of changing conditions, and their interest in political theory developed essentially out of the need to defend their policies and methods against the increasing criticism of political opponents. The constitutional thought of men like Kido Koin, Okubo Toshimichi, Ito Hirobumi, and Iwakura Tomomi crystallized in a period when modernization was seriously challenged by reactionary rebellions and when authoritarianism was attacked by Itagaki Taisuke and Goto Shojiro, both jealous of the monopoly of political power held by Satsuma and Choshu.

An interest in constitutional government had developed among samurai-intellectuals during the latter part of the Tokugawa period, when there were numerous proposals for reform of the feudal system. As early as 1843, the *daimyo* of Echizen ordered Sugida Seikei to translate the Dutch constitution. Shortly thereafter the *Bakufu* established the *Bansho shirabedokoro,* some members of which translated and studied Western works on constitutional government. The overthrow of the Tokugawa Shogunate further stimulated discussions of political theory, and samurai-intellectuals looked eagerly to the Western world for lessons in the practical operation of constitutional government. Intellectuals like Kato Hiroyuki and Fukuzawa Yukichi, who sought to find the sources of strength in Western society, were attracted by principles of liberty and representative government and did much to popularize these concepts among the Japanese.[1] These ideas were quickly seized upon and expounded by such political opponents of the Satsuma-Choshu oligarchs as Itagaki and his followers.

The oligarchs were also interested in Western political theory, but in the first few years of the Meiji era leaders like Kido and Okubo were forced to adopt a pragmatic approach to the problem of government. They were intent upon the establishment of an effective centralized administration. While they tended to regard constitutional government as a vague, distant goal, they were careful to initiate studies of Western political thought. Thus in 1869 the government appointed a special committee, headed by Eto Shimpei, to carry out an investigation of Western constitutions,[2] and, after the government reorganization of 1871, the *Sain* was for a time the center of a lively discussion concerning the establishment of a constitution and parliament.[3]

Kido Koin, who accompanied Iwakura on his mission to Europe and the United States in 1871, had the opportunity to observe Western constitutional government in operation and was the first major political leader to become convinced that the government of Japan should be based upon a written constitution. Kido expressed this view during the political crisis of 1873 when the issue was war with Korea. He defended the policy of priority for domestic reform and modernization against the alternative policy of foreign expansion and, like several of his colleagues, he became increasingly concerned with the general problem of government organization. Kido submitted a memorial which urged

---

1. Osatake, *Nihon kensei shi taiko*, I, 278. For a list of important works regarding political theory and government written in the early years of the Meiji era, see Osatake, *Ishin zengo ni okeru rikken shiso*, II, 223.
2. Suzuki Yasuzo, *Nihon kempo shi gaisetsu* (Tokyo, 1941), 43-46.
3. For documents relating to the constitutional discussions of the *Sain*, see Fujii Jintaro, *Nihon kempo seitei shi* (Tokyo, 1929), 130-132. See also Miyakoshi, *Nihon kensei kiso shiryo*, 83-84, 85-86. For secondary accounts, see Miyajima Seiichiro, "Kokken hensan kigen" in *Meiji bunka zenshu*, IV, 343-347, and Suzuki Yasuzo, *Meiji shonen no rikken shiso* (Tokyo, 1938), 3-33.

THE MAKING OF THE MEIJI CONSTITUTION

that a constitution be established to provide a legal foundation for the powers and structure of the government.[4] He extolled constitutional government that was responsible to the will of the people; however, he pointed out that the people of Japan had not reached this level of political development. Thus the situation required at best a gradual approach to the establishment of popular participation in the processes of government; in the meantime, the Emperor and his officials, the Satsuma-Choshu oligarchy, would carry on the administration on behalf of the people.

The advocates of priority for modernization, whose victory in the war question was a narrow but decisive one, approved Kido's suggestion to consider the matter of establishing a constitution. In November 1873, the government appointed Ito Hirobumi and Terajima Munenori to make a general study of constitutional government.[5] To facilitate their work, Ito first consulted with Kido.

Kido summarized his views in a list of general principles which he submitted to Ito.[6] These suggestions seem to be based upon a draft constitution that Kido had ordered Aoki Shuzo to compile in 1872.[7] Kido reiterated his conviction that a constitution was essential for the achievement of efficiency in national as well as local administration; however, he continued to feel that constitutional government had to evolve gradually. In reply to the demands for the immediate establishment of a representative assembly, Kido warned against rash action to "Europeanize" the government. Although he conceded the inevitability of a bicameral legislative system, he insisted that, for the time being, the government had to exercise both administrative and legislative power. Kido was keenly aware of the need for strong leadership to carry out the program of domestic reform and modernization;

---

4. "Discourse of Kido Takayoshi upon his return to Japan in 1873" in McLaren, *Japanese Government Documents*, 567-577.
5. Osatake, *Nihon kensei shi taiko*, I, 317.
6. A list of these suggestions is included in Osatake, *Nihon kensei shi taiko*, I, 317-318.
7. See Osatake's discussion of the authorship of the draft, *ibid.*, 319-324. The draft is reproduced in full, 324-345. A translation is included herein as Appendix I.

consequently, he was satisfied to have political power remain in the hands of the Councillors of State *(Sangi)* and the ministers of the various departments.

The ultimate constitutional system that Kido envisioned was a monarchial one based upon broad imperial powers. However, Kido urged that the fundamental law of Japan ought not to be despotic, although he conceded that it would be difficult to avoid despotism in the fields of education and the military. He thought in terms of a monarchy whose power would be limited generally by strict adherence to a constitution and specifically by a system of limited ministerial responsibility to parliament. In the final analysis, Kido regarded a constitution as a means to secure and maintain harmony between the powers of the Emperor's government and the rights of the people.

Kido's draft constitution, which was written in great detail, confirmed the Emperor as the fountainhead of political power.[8] The Emperor would have power to superintend the administration, to conduct foreign policy, and to command the army and navy; consequently, the Emperor would appoint and dismiss all officials, declare war and make peace, and conclude treaties. With regard to legislation, the Emperor would have the right to veto all bills passed by parliament; moreover, he would be vested with the power to issue emergency ordinances that would have the force of law. However, an imperial ordinance would require the countersignature of a minister who would bear personal responsibility to parliament for its provisions. When the government declared a national emergency, the Ministers of State as a body would assume responsibility for the announcement and would explain the circumstances to parliament when it reconvened.

While these powers resided in the person of the Emperor, they would be exercised by his ministers who would actually

---

8. The articles of the constitution are divided as follows: National boundaries, 324; Rights and duties of citizens, 324-330; Affairs of state, 330-331; Powers of the Emperor, 331-334; Powers and responsibilities of Ministers, 334-335; *Genroin,* 335-336; Powers of the *Giin,* 336-339; Local government, 339-343; Officials, 343-344; General provisions, 344-345.

manage the administration in accordance with the constitution. Kido envisioned some sort of cabinet headed by a Prime Minister *(Dajodaijin)*, and he did not seem to limit the powers of this body by any comprehensive system of ministerial responsibility to parliament. Instead, his draft merely stated that a minister might be censured by parliament and dismissed from office for misconduct or violation of the constitution. It is interesting to note that Kido provided for special cabinet posts for elder statesmen *(genro)*. He also supported the principle of the division of responsibility between the civil government and the military; consequently, he stipulated that the Ministers of the Army and the Navy would be appointed exclusively from among military and naval officers.

Kido also outlined provisions for a bicameral parliament, which would share legislative power with the Emperor. Actually, parliament's role in formulating legislation would be severely limited by the imperial veto power and emergency ordinance power. The Emperor would also have the right to dissolve parliament in emergencies, although in the case of dissolution, a new parliament would have to be selected within six months. The articles regarding the upper house *(Genroin)* simply stated that it would assist the Emperor in an advisory legislative capacity. As for its members, they would be appointed by the Emperor from among officials of the *chokunin* rank, who paid annual taxes of at least two hundred and ten yen.

Kido discussed the lower house *(Giin)* in much greater detail. The members would represent the people as a whole and discuss affairs of state to help formulate legislation. They would be instructed to express their views openly and vote in the interests of the people. All sessions of the lower house would be public unless a secret session should be necessitated by circumstances. Although Kido conceded that the majority of the members of the lower house should be elected by the people, for the time being all would be appointed by the Emperor. Twenty-nine court nobles *(kuge)* would have permanent seats; the remainder of the membership would be selected from among high officials in the prefectural administration, particularly governors.

While the role of the lower house in drafting legislation would be hardly more than an advisory one, it would have several important financial powers that it might exploit. For example, the annual budget of the government would require the consent of the lower house. The draft constitution also stipulated that the annual expenditures of the imperial family would be decided by law and paid out of tax revenues; moreover, the lower house would determine what constituted the private property (lands, money, castles, etc.) of the imperial family. Finally, whenever it would be necessary to amend the constitution, the government or parliament might initiate action which would require the approval of both houses of parliament.

Kido's treatment of judicial power and the court system was introduced by the general statement that the power to enact legal principles and adjudge cases would reside in the courts. Although he expected the court system to be worked out in detail by legislation, he did provide for three classes of courts: a supreme court in Tokyo, circuit courts for groups of prefectures, and local courts on the district (*gun*) level.

Kido discussed the rights and duties of citizens at great length. He reaffirmed such social reforms as freedom of occupation and residence which had put an end to old feudal customs. He added the fundamental principles that "all Japanese are legally equal regardless of rank" and "to each person there are reserved certain inherent rights conferred by heaven." These he listed as freedom from illegal arrest, search, and seizure of property, the right to a fair trial, freedom of speech, freedom of assembly, and the freedom to petition and complain to the government. Kido condemned partiality in the appointment of citizens to political office and stated that all citizens, according to their ability, should have the right to hold office in the government.

Kido included several important qualifications with regard to these basic freedoms. For example, freedom of speech did not contain the right to slander the government or fellow citizens. Publishers of newspapers and journals would be required to secure permission to publish and would be held responsible for opinions in their publications. Police permission would be necessary for the convocation of large outdoor meetings. Of course, in time of war, all these freedoms might be suspended by law in whole or in part. Kido seemingly did not accept the principle of religious freedom: he stated that Buddhism would be the national faith of Japan while Christianity and other religions ought to be prohibited. All citizens had two important obligations, military service according to the regulations of the army and navy and payment of taxes.

Kido's so-called "gradual approach" to the problem of constitutional government can be seen in his provisions regarding local government[9] and education. The draft constitution stated that the Emperor would have the power to appoint all local officials except the heads of *kumi,* who would be elected by the local inhabitants; however, Kido's great interest in developing local self-government was reflected in several articles which provided for popular discussion of important local affairs such as taxes by local assemblies. Kido felt that every male Japanese was entitled to an education; no doubt, this conviction was based upon the idea that the political enlightenment of the masses was an absolute prerequisite for their participation in the processes of government. Thus the draft constitution provided for a national public school system and compulsory attendance at the elementary school level. Kido went so far as to promise that the government would enable all boys, however poor, to get an elementary education. This school system would be directed by the central government, which would have the power to appoint public school teachers who would serve as minor officials of the government. Kido also recognized the

---

9. Aoki Shuzo, a student in Germany at this time, was influenced by the Prussian system of government and advocated to Kido the establishment of a well-organized local administration before setting up a constitution. For his views, see Miyakoshi, *Nihon kensei kiso shiryo,* 125-126.

value of private schools, so long as their curricula would be approved by the Ministry of Education.

Kido's views went unheeded. The less conciliatory Okubo, who came to dominate the government more and more, held to the opinion that the central administration should establish a constitution that was based on the current *Dajokan* system.[10] Okubo felt that, because Japan was in a period of transition from feudalism to a modern national state, some form of imperial absolutism was essential for the time being to protect the nation against foreign pressures and to enable Japan to reach a position of equality with the great powers. He was particularly attracted by Prussian concepts of government as well as the dynamic leadership of Bismarck. In Okubo's mind, an absolute government dominated by men of ability was in keeping with Japanese tradition as well as the conditions of the times. Ito, increasingly influenced by Okubo, supported this view completely.[11]

Okubo did concede that the Japanese people were becoming more and more concerned with politics and that the establishment of a constitution was inevitable. He regarded constitutional monarchy as the ultimate form of government for Japan, but he too did not think in terms of responsible parliamentary government. Okubo was convinced that democratic, representative government was not suitable to the customs and needs of Japan. In his mind, the function of a constitution was to "establish harmony between the ruler and the people by fixing the powers of the Emperor and limiting the rights of the people." However, government would no longer be completely arbitrary since officials would govern according to the basic law of the land. Okubo seemed to feel that both the nation as a whole and the people required the continued guidance of authoritarian government, and he was extremely wary of possible encroachments upon the

---

10. For the constitutional views of Okubo, see Osatake, *Nihon kensei shi taiko*, I, 345-361. A translation is included as Appendix II.
11. Miyakoshi, *Nihon kensei kiso shiryo*, 123-125. It is interesting to note that Okubo recommended to Ito that he consult with Fukuzawa Yukichi. Ito, who detested the liberal views of Fukuzawa, rejected the proposal. Osatake, *Ishin zengo ni okeru rikken shiso*, II, 71-72.

powers of the Emperor and his ministers by a parliament. He insisted that political power remain in the hands of a small group of able leaders, assisting the Emperor who was the source of all power. He regarded his views as a middle way between representative government and arbitrary imperial absolutism. Thus Okubo would preserve the *Dajokan* system as the nucleus of Japan's ultimate constitutional government. He would establish a legislative body, but it would be appointed and only advisory.

The leaders of the defeated "war party" found it impossible to remain in the government. Saigo Takamori, Itagaki, Goto, and Eto resigned from the *Dajokan* Council, and Soejima left the Foreign Office. Their resignations ended any pretension of a four-*han* coalition government, since the new government was characterized by greater concentration of power in the hands of the members of the "peace party." Saigo, as ideological leader of a great part of the ex-samurai, retired to Satsuma, where he continued to oppose the program of rapid modernization. Itagaki and Goto began to organize political-party opposition to the authoritarian government from which they were excluded. To the leaders of the government, the challenge of a conservative opposition to modernization was more fundamental, especially since it was likely to be based upon the military power of the discontented ex-samurai. This assumption proved to be true, for beginning in 1874 numerous local revolts led by ex-samurai broke out throughout Japan, while in the background there lurked the threat of a united armed opposition under the leadership of Saigo and Satsuma.

Under these circumstances, Okubo and his followers were forced to modify their views. As a result, Okubo made a determined effort to persuade Kido, who had resigned in opposition to the Formosan expedition,[12] and Itagaki to rejoin the govern-

---

12. Kido's ill health resulted in a decline of his influence in the government since he was unable to attend many sessions of the *Dajokan;* moreover, his resignation in 1874 over the Formosan expedition temporarily left Okubo as the unchallenged leader within the government. Kido opposed the expedition on the same grounds as war with Korea, and criticized Okubo for using Formosa as a compromise with the "war party" and as a means of diverting attention from the problems of domestic politics. Fujii and Moriya, *Sogo nihon shi taikei*, 494-495.

ment in order to get a maximum of support for the administration. In January 1875, Okubo confided his intentions to Ito, who proposed a reorganization of the government in order to persuade Kido and Itagaki to rejoin it. Ito's proposals were, in fact, an acceptance of Kido's emphasis upon the *gradual* development of constitutional government; moreover, they appear to have been based upon Kido's draft constitution. They provided for the establishment of an appointed Senate *(Genroin)* and a lower house of prefectural governors *(Chihokankaigi)* in preparation for a national parliament, the creation of a Supreme Court *(Daishinin)* as the nucleus of an independent judiciary, and a functional division of the *Dajokan* into a cabinet responsible for the formation of policy and the various departments responsible for the administration of that policy. Kido and Itagaki met with Okubo in February 1875; they accepted Ito's proposals and agreed to resume office in the government.[13]

By March 28, a committee made up of Okubo, Ito, Kido, and Itagaki completed a plan for the reorganization of the government and, on April 14, their draft was made official by an imperial rescript which promised that "constitutional government would be established in gradual stages."[14] The *Sain* and *Uin* were abolished, and only the *Seiin* was retained as the policy-making cabinet of the *Dajokan*. In theory, the new government was based upon the "separation of powers," with the *Dajokan* as the supreme executive body exercising power in the name of the Emperor, the *Genroin* and the *Chihokankaigi* as a bicameral legislature, and the *Daishinin* as the judiciary. However, the *Dajokan* was scarcely changed and remained the focal point of the oligarchy's power.

The *Genroin* proved to be nothing more than an advisory body whose main function was to deliberate upon bills submitted

---
13. *Ibid.*, 506.
14. For the text of this document, see Miyakoshi, *Nihon kensei kiso shiryo*, 186. The English translation which appears in McLaren, *Japanese Government Documents*, 41-42, omits this promise.

by the *Dajokan,* which had the power to indicate whether these bills were for decision or simply for study and discussion; moreover, the *Dajokan* continued to have the power to issue legislation on its own authority, having only to submit its measures for the inspection of the *Genroin.*[15] Almost immediately after its creation, the *Genroin* became a center of political controversy between the various factions that made up the *Dajokan.* Itagaki and his followers worked for the transformation of the *Genroin* into an effective legislative organ of the government; however, the oligarchs continued to maintain the arbitrary legislative power of the *Dajokan.* Kido defended this latter view and emphasized gradual political reform through the expansion of popular education and the development of local self-government.[16] On the side of extreme conservatism, Iwakura Tomomi considered the *Genroin* to be incompatible with the system of imperial government; consequently, he opposed the whole reorganization plan, did not attend the sessions of the *Dajokan,* and offered to resign his official post.[17]

The meetings of the *Chihokankaigi* were merely convocations of prefectural governors in routine administrative conferences[18]

---

15. McLaren, *Japanese Government Documents,* 43-45.

16. Fujii and Moriya, *Sogo nihon shi taikei,* 513-514.

17. In his resignation, which the Emperor refused to accept, Iwakura concluded that "the *Genroin* would destroy the great accomplishment of re-establishing the imperial system." Osatake, *Nihon kensei shi taiko,* II, 392.

18. McLaren, *Japanese Government Documents,* 505-512. As early as April 1873, the Department of Finance, acting on the advice of Inouye Kaoru, had issued regulations for the calling of a conference of local officials to discuss economic matters of local and national importance. This conference, which convened on April 8, 1873, caused a minor crisis because the leaders of the government feared that the Department of Finance might emerge as the dominant force in the government. The matter was easily resolved, however, when Inouye resigned over a financial decision and the government put an end to this conference. When the idea of an assembly of local officials persisted, the government, with the approval of Itagaki and Saigo, proposed the establishment of an assembly of *fu* and *ken* governors. However, it was not until March 1874 that an imperial rescript announced that the government intended to create such a body in response to the January memorial of Itagaki and his followers. On May 2, 1874, the government issued rules and regulations for the *Chihokankaigi* and stated that the date of its first convocation would be announced shortly thereafter. However, because of several postponements, the *Chihokankaigi* was not convened until June 1875, when it assumed the role of the lower house in the reorganized government.

under the control of the Home Minister. When it was convened in June 1875, Goto Shojiro, Vice-President of the *Genroin,* criticized the *Chihokankaigi* as "merely participating in the Emperor's power to frame laws and not being a legislative body in any sense." Ito replied to this charge for the government, stating that "the *Chihokankaigi* was a step on the way to popular representation in a national assembly."[19] The concept of an independent judiciary met a similar fate since the *Daishinin* was placed under the control of the *Dajokan* through regulations which directly subordinated it to the Department of Justice.

During 1875 and most of 1876, the main stumbling block to successful reorganization of the government proved to be the problem of dividing the functions of the *Dajokan*. Kido and Itagaki had re-entered the government on the condition that the executive and administrative functions of the *Dajokan* would be separated. They had both objected to the practice whereby Councillors of State were at the same time ministers of the various departments.[20] However, their objections were ignored and the majority of the Councillors of the reorganized government continued to serve as ministers of departments. In a memorial to the Emperor, Itagaki protested that this was a violation of the agreement he had made with Okubo, but only Shimazu Hisamitsu, ex-*daimyo* of Satsuma who had been persuaded to rejoin the government, sided with him. On October 19, 1876, the Emperor stated that there would be no division of the executive and administrative functions of the *Dajokan*.[21] On the very day that the government promulgated the Emperor's decision, Shimazu presented a memorial which criticized the Councillors for their policies de-

---

19. Osatake, *Nihon kensei shi taiko*, II, 426-427. Osatake feels that the protests of Goto and Itagaki were really based upon their desire to monopolize legislative power through a single-house system based on the *Genroin*. See the proposals of Goto and Itagaki, *ibid.*, 394-397.

20. It is interesting to note that the supremacy of Okubo rested to a great extent on the fact that he was not only a Councillor of State but also Minister of Home Affairs, a post which gave him control over the whole system of local government.

21. Fujii and Moriya, *Sogo nihon shi taikei*, 517. Until this time, Okubo had used the excuse of a crisis with Korea to postpone action on this matter.

THE MAKING OF THE MEIJI CONSTITUTION

signed to modernize Japan.[22] Both Itagaki and Shimazu presented their resignations and, although the government feared the loss of these men, the resignations were accepted on October 27, 1876. Thus the attempt by Okubo and Ito to broaden the basis of the government's support ended in failure. The oligarchy received an additional blow in the following year, when Kido died after a long illness.

---

22. Okubo continued to be concerned about the lack of Satsuma support for his policies, and he devoted his attention to trying to persuade both Shimazu Hisamitsu and Saigo to resume office in the government. While Shimazu did return to the government temporarily as *Sadaijin* in compliance with an imperial order, Saigo remained at Kagoshima where he conducted a private school to train ex-samurai in government and military science. Shimazu continued to attack the government's policy of centralization and modernization and urged a return "to the good old days." Fujii and Moriya, *Sogo nihon shi taikei*, 496-504.

Chapter IV
The Oligarchy and the Democratic Movement, 1876-1881

The political settlement of 1875 was the beginning of a government policy of compromise with the leaders of the so-called "democratic movement." This policy, alternating with one of vigorous suppression of political opponents, was continued through the decade of the 1870's and later. From 1876 to 1881 its high points were the draft constitutions of the *Genroin* and the establishment of local assemblies in 1878. As a compromise policy, it tended to utilize the views of Kido Koin, who had advocated a line of political development that was a middle course between the demands of the Tosa faction led by Itagaki and the steadfast absolutism of the oligarchs who sought to maintain their monopoly of political power. The oligarchs utilized Kido's proposals because of the mounting political pressures of the times—the threat of a widespread reactionary rebellion by ex-samurai under the leadership of Satsuma and Saigo as well as increasing criticism by Itagaki and Goto, who were rapidly gaining the support of discontented elements among the masses. However, the oligarchs failed to prevent the Satsuma Rebellion; nor were they able to halt the transformation of Tosa factional discontent into a popularly based democratic movement.

While Kido seems to have been sincere in trying to effect a synthesis of the imperial system and representative government, Okubo and his colleagues were only interested in protecting the imperial system and their own power. They did not seem to have any long range program of political development in mind. Those changes in government that the oligarchs did implement in this period were the result of the practical necessity to compromise with their political enemies.

The government, which regarded Saigo's ambitions as the more immediate and pressing threat to its power, began to take

THE MAKING OF THE MEIJI CONSTITUTION

steps in the fall of 1876 to strengthen its control over Kagoshima, with the result that, in February 1877, Saigo and his followers finally resorted to a test of arms to gain greater power for themselves and Satsuma. This rebellion, which the government suppressed with great difficulty by the following September, proved to be the last armed revolt by the ex-samurai, who shortly thereafter disintegrated as a separate class. The victory of the government's conscript army had wiped out the last territorial base for an attack against the regime. Another important result of the Satsuma Rebellion was the confirmation of coöperation between the oligarchs of Satsuma and Choshu. The suppression of the rebellion in no way impaired the influence of Satsuma officials in the government; on the contrary, leaders from the two former *han* continued to work in harmony. They established a more definite balance of power among themselves and tightened their monopoly of political power against opponents.[1]

The Satsuma Rebellion also marks a definite change in the leadership of the government, for, by the spring of 1878, the original triumvirate of the Meiji Revolution, Okubo, Kido, and Saigo, had ceased to exist. Kido had died on May 26, 1877; Saigo perished in September 1877 by his own hand in the last battle of the rebellion; and Okubo fell before an assassin on May 14, 1878. From 1878 on, Ito, Okuma, Terajima, Matsukata, Kuroda, and Yamagata emerged as the most important leaders in the government; Iwakura Tomomi remained as the spokesman for an intensely conservative political philosophy which sought to resist any political reform that would impair the power of the Emperor.[2]

---

1. This does not mean that a feeling of rivalry did not continue to exist between Satsuma and Choshu. In fact, in 1878, after the death of Okubo, Satsuma leaders sought to form a coalition with Okuma and his followers; when this failed Matsukata, who had assumed leadership of Satsuma political interests, hurried home from Paris to prevent Inouye Kaoru from assuming office as Minister of Finance. Since Ito was Minister of Home Affairs, the leaders of Satsuma felt that another key post should not fall to Choshu. Inouye's appointment was blocked, and the post fell to Okuma, who continued to ignore requests from Satsuma for a political alliance. Fujii and Moriya, *Sogo nihon shi taikei,* 586-587.
2. For a list of the personnel who filled the most important posts in the government after the death of Okubo, see Fujii and Moriya, *Sogo nihon shi taikei,* 585.

The Democratic Movement, 1876-1881

Armed rebellion had come to an end with the failure of the Satsuma Rebellion and the death of Saigo; however, Itagaki and his followers continued to criticize the authoritarian nature of the government, and they worked constantly to make their opposition more effective by enlarging its mass support. On the whole, the leaders of this democratic movement took a neutral position during the Satsuma Rebellion; Itagaki insisted upon achieving his aims through the pressure of public opinion. But he did regard the rebellion as an excellent opportunity to press the government to accept the demands of his group.[3] Thus in June 1877, the *Risshisha* memorialized the government to establish a national parliament; at the same time, the memorial was printed and circulated throughout Japan. The memorialists complained that the political disunity of the country was occasioned by the "despotism of the government oligarchy which carried on the administration without reference to the opinion of the nation." They based their demand for the convocation of a parliament on the *Charter Oath* of 1868 and criticized the government for its failure to implement the "separation of powers" outlined in the imperial rescript of 1875. The government, occupied with the suppression of the Satsuma Rebellion, promptly rejected these demands.[4]

After the suppression of the Satsuma Rebellion, the demand for popular rights became widespread, and the government was confronted with increased criticism and agitation for a parliament. Locally, the leadership of the democratic movement began to give way to non-samurai, passing into the hands of the rural landlord-industrialists, and mass support was gained among discontented peasants and wage earners. The principal organ of this movement was the *Aikokusha;* this national political party was

---

3. There was a group among his followers who sought to achieve its aims by force. To men like Hayashi Yuzo and Oe Taku, the Satsuma Rebellion was an unequalled opportunity for armed action. Their plot was discovered by the government and the leaders were arrested and imprisoned. Later, however, they were pardoned and in the cases of Kataoka Kenkichi and Mutsu Munemitsu were invited to serve in the government.

4. McLaren, *Japanese Government Documents,* 457-480. The memorial was drafted by Yoshida Masaharu, Ueki Emori, and Takeuchi Ko.

formed by the leaders of the *Risshisha* at Osaka in September 1878, and, within a short time, numerous local affiliates, which worked to stir up the peasantry, arose on the village level. In order to coördinate the activities of the various local political parties, in March 1879 the leaders of the *Aikokusha* called a national convention at Osaka, which was attended by a total of eighty delegates. In November 1879, a second convention resolved to petition the Emperor for a national parliament. By the time the third convention met in March 1880, political agitation reached such proportions that the leaders of the government decided to take action; on April 5, they passed a law restricting public meetings and issued a decree ordering the convention to disband.[5]

Forewarned of the actions that the government was planning, the leaders of the convention resolved to continue their activities until their aims were achieved. Kataoka Kenkichi and Kono Hironaka were sent to Tokyo to petition the Emperor for a parliament. The oligarchs refused to accept the petition and informed the bearers that all petitions should be submitted to the local prefectural governments, which would transmit them to the *Genroin*.[6]

During these years when the democratic movement reached its peak, the oligarchs vainly attempted to meet the demands of the opposition with a policy of compromise based upon the establishment of local elected assemblies. Actually, local assemblies had been formed in several *han* in the early 1870's through the initiative of local officials, and after 1872 they were functioning in many prefectures.[7] In 1875, the representatives of thirteen prefectures met and submitted a memorial to the *Chihokankaigi* requesting the creation of prefectural assemblies on a national scale. They argued that such institutions would provide forums to

---

5. Miyakoshi, *Nihon kensei kiso shiryo*, 258.
6. During 1880 at least fifty-five petitions were presented to the government urging the establishment of a parliament. Osatake Takeki, *Nihon kensei shi* (Tokyo, 1930). 260-264.
7. Fujii, *Nihon kempo seitei shi*, 143. Between 1871-1879, assemblies were established in forty-eight prefectures. For a list of these assemblies, see Osatake, *Nihon kensei shi taiko*, I, 267.

THE DEMOCRATIC MOVEMENT, 1876-1881

develop popular experience in government.[8] Finally, during the first session of the *Chihokankaigi*, which was opened by the Emperor in June 1875, the government submitted a draft of regulations for prefectural *(ken)* and urban *(fu)* assemblies and asked the *Chihokankaigi* to decide whether members of such assemblies should be local government officials or elected representatives.[9] After a lively discussion, a vote of the *Chihokankaigi* was taken, and a majority recommended the establishment of local assemblies composed of local government officials.[10]

Before the government was able to put these regulations into operation, it was confronted by the samurai revolts of 1876 and 1877, but after their suppression the oligarchs again turned to the matter of local assemblies. In order to offset the demands of the formidable democratic movement, they submitted a draft of regulations for popularly elected prefectural and urban assemblies to the second session of the *Chihokankaigi*, which was convened in April 1878.[11] A majority of that body voted to approve the government's draft with one exception, to reduce the voting qualification based upon the land tax from ten yen to five yen.[12] In July 1878, these regulations were promulgated by the government.

Shortly thereafter, the government established prefectural and urban assemblies which would be convened for one month each year and on special occasions. Male subjects, with the exception of public school teachers, military men, lunatics, and criminals, over twenty-five years of age, who paid a land-tax of at least five yen per year, became eligible to vote.[13] Male subjects, with the same exceptions, over twenty-five years of age, who paid a land-tax of at least ten yen per year, were eligible for assembly membership in the prefecture in which they lived. As for their legislative power,

---

8. For the text of this memorial see Osatake, *Nihon kensei shi taiko*, I, 262-263.
9. Fujii, *Nihon kempo seitei shi*, 160.
10. *Ibid.*, 167. The debate in the *Chihokankaigi* is summarized, 161-165.
11. *Ibid.*, 204-205.
12. For a summary of the debate on the second draft, see *ibid.*, 205-210.
13. McLaren, *Japanese Government Documents*, 272-276. In 1880, the age limit was lowered to twenty. *Ibid.*, 292.

THE MAKING OF THE MEIJI CONSTITUTION

the assemblies were only permitted to deliberate upon bills submitted by the governor, who had veto power over their decisions.[14]

Although these assemblies were criticized widely because they were powerless to check the local bureaucratic controls of the central government, they did serve as forums for political agitation by the leaders of the democratic movement who used them to popularize their views. The oligarchs, on the other hand, expanded the policy of concessions; in 1880 they extended the establishment of popularly elected assemblies to cities, towns, and villages.[15] These local assemblies were modeled on the prefectural assemblies and as such were no more acceptable to the leaders of the democratic movement. Matters for discussion were submitted by the local officials appointed by the central government, who also had the power to suspend the decisions of the assemblies or call upon the prefectural governors to suspend or dissolve the assemblies. In such instances, the local official had the power to enact legislation which was subject to the approval of the governor.

During this period the government was also careful to control the organs of public opinion, particularly the press. Modern Japanese newspapers began to be published shortly after the Meiji Restoration, and they soon became an important factor in politics as a means of mobilizing public opinion. By 1873 the press of Japan had taken sides in the political issues that divided the government and the Tosa faction; and in that year the oligarchs began to take firm measures to control newspaper attacks against their policies. In October, they issued a Press Law[16] which

---

14. By 1880, the assemblies proved to be the scene of numerous conflicts between local governors and the members who agitated for increased power. In an attempt to lessen friction, the government provided for mediation by the Home Minister and in the case of financial matters by the Minister of Finance. *Ibid.,* 288. In 1881, a Board of Adjudication was established in the *Dajokan* to settle disputes between the governors and the assemblies. However, because of the increasing intractability of several assemblies which refused to discuss bills or finish their deliberations, the governors were permitted to put measures into operation on the approval of the Home Minister. *Ibid.,* 302, 309.

15. *Ibid.,* 296-297.

16. *Ibid.,* 534-535. For the beginnings of government moves in this direction, see *ibid.,* 529-530, 530-532, 532-533.

made it necessary for newspapers to secure official authorization to publish and prohibited editorial attacks upon the government, discussion of laws, or attempts to "cast obstacles in the way of the working of national institutions by persistent advocacy of foreign ideas." Moreover, the press was forbidden to comment upon officials of the government during their term of office.

When this law proved to be ineffective as a means of controlling the press, Okubo secured its repeal in 1875 and replaced it with a more drastic measure that made slander and criticism of the government and its officials a crime punishable by imprisonment or fine.[17] According to the new law, the editor of a newspaper as well as the writer would be held responsible for offenses committed by the newspaper.[18] During 1875 and 1876, as a direct result of the application of this regulation, the government arrested sixty editors and newspapermen. Between 1876 and 1880, fines and jail sentences, based upon alleged slander and libel, were common, since the press persisted in attacking the limited legislative power of the newly created local assemblies.[19]

By 1880, the government also moved to restrict public meetings and to hinder, if not prevent, the development of political parties. It passed a law[20] which stipulated that a public political meeting or discussion required an official permit and authorized the police to exercise control over such meetings with the power to dissolve them. Political societies were forbidden to "combine or communicate with other societies," while "men in the armed forces, teachers and students, and policemen were prohibited from attending political meetings or becoming members of political parties."

The enforcement of these repressive laws required vigorous action by the Japanese police, who were organized under the

---

17. *Ibid.*, 539-540.
18. Areas of possible libelous offenses or subversion of the state were listed as follows: ". . . in every case where the discussion turns upon foreign or domestic politics, finance, feelings of the nation, the aspect of the times, learning or religion, or matters affecting the rights of officials or people," *ibid.*, 541.
19. In July 1877, the Press Law of 1875 was amended to invest the Home Minister with the power to suppress or delay the publication of a newspaper.
20. *Ibid.*, 495-499.

control of the Home Minister;[21] the government did not hesitate to use the police against the democratic movement. The Tokyo police were directed to "search out and punish those guilty of political offenses."[22] The government was especially concerned over the possible spread of democratic thought in the army and, when a unit of the Imperial Guard mutinied in 1878 because of an arrears in pay, the government suspected that the troops had been influenced by the political attacks of the democratic movement. Shortly thereafter, to reinforce military discipline, General Yamagata issued a general warning to the members of the army to abstain from the discussion of politics.[23]

Yet, in the period 1876-1881 the government did not overlook the problem of drawing up a constitution.[24] As early as September 1876, the government established the *Kempo Seido Torishirabe Kyoku* (Bureau to Study the Establishment of a Constitution) under the chairmanship of Prince Arisugawa Taruhito, President of the *Genroin,* who was ordered by the Emperor to supervise the drafting of a constitution.[25] It is perhaps noteworthy that the Emperor presented Prince Arisugawa with a copy of

---

21. Local police were superintended by governors of prefectures and urban areas (*fu*), who were responsible to the Home Minister. The Tokyo Metropolitan Police Office was placed directly under the Department of Home Affairs. By 1877, both the national police system and the Tokyo police were placed under a Chief Police Inspector in the Department of Home Affairs.

22. *Ibid.,* 257.

23. Yamagata Aritomo, "Gunjin Kunkai" ("Admonitions to Soldiers"), *Meiji bunka zenshu,* XIII, 100. In 1881, the government increased its supervision over the army by the creation of a gendarmerie (*kempeitai*) to discover and root out dissident thought in the army.

24. This section is concerned principally with the efforts of the government to compile a constitution between the years 1876-1881. However, during this period, there was an equally great concern among private individuals and organizations, many of which presented draft constitutions to the government. Societies were formed especially for this purpose, and some of the drafts were printed in the press. On the whole, the efforts of private indivduals serve to reveal the great differences between the ideas that prevailed among the liberal groups and those of the oligarchs. For a summary of these developments, see Fujii, *Nihon kempo seitei shi,* 228-229. For the texts of several of the private drafts, see *Meiji bunka zenshu,* III, 377-416.

25. The imperial order stated: "We hereby desire that a constitution which is based on the system established at the time of the founding of the nation and which gives due consideration to the laws of the various nations be drafted." Osatake, *Nihon kensei shi taiko,* II, 460. The other members of the committee were Nakashima Nobuyuki, Yanagihara Sakimitsu, Hosokawa Junjiro, and Fukuba Bisei. Miyakoshi, *Nihon kensei kiso shiryo,* 19.

The Democratic Movement, 1876-1881

Todd's *Parliamentary Government in England*.[26] However, the committee did not confine its study to British parliamentary practice; the members discussed eleven other systems of constitutional government including France, Italy, Prussia, and Austria.[27]

Between September 1876 and May 1878, the *Genroin* committee compiled four draft constitutions, the last of which was submitted to the government for its consideration.[28] On the whole, the *Genroin* draft constitution made an important concession to the democratic movement in that it provided for certain constitutional checks upon the Emperor, whose powers would no longer be unlimited. He would continue to conduct the administration through his ministers, with specific power to command the army and navy, to declare war, to make peace, and to conclude treaties, but with certain limitations in the form of special responsibilities to parliament. For example, the draft constitution provided that "those treaties which would involve expenditures or a change in the national boundary would require the approval of both houses of parliament." The oligarchs regarded this as an unnecessary limitation upon the powers of the Emperor, but they were much more critical of the provision that "the annual income of the Emperor would be decided by law," since this attacked his financial independence.

It was in the matter of legislative power, however, that the draft constitution made the greatest inroads on the absolute power of the Emperor, for it provided that the legislative power would be "shared by the Emperor and the parliament." While bills

---

26. Alpheus Todd, *On Parliamentary Government in England: Its Origin, Development and Practical Operation* (London, 1866) had been brought from England by Yoshii Tomozane and shown to Okubo and Ito, both of whom expressed very little enthusiasm for it. Osatake, *Nihon kensei shi taiko*, II, 460-461.

27. Asai explains that although they used England as a working model, they modified its system of parliamentary government by adding constitutional practices of other states. It is interesting to note that all of the states studied, with the exception of France, were constitutional monarchies and that the committee did not consult the constitutions of the United States, the German Empire, or Switzerland, all of which were federations in structure. Asai Kiyoshi, *Genroin no kempo hensan temmatsu* (Tokyo, 1946), 38-39.

28. The following discussion is based upon the text of this draft which is included in Asai, *op. cit.*, 72-86, and Osatake, *Nihon kensei shi taiko*, II, 464-478. A translation is included as Appendix III.

would be submitted to parliament by the Emperor, who would have the ultimate power of veto, "all bills would require the consent of both houses." The only exception to this rule would be the budget and tax measures, both of which would require the consent of only the lower house. The parliament would also participate in the process of constitutional amendment, for the draft provided that "amendment would require the consent of both houses expressed by at least a two-thirds majority."

Parliament would consist of the *Genroin* and the *Daigishiin* (House of Representatives). The *Genroin* would be largely a continuation of the body already in existence with its members chosen from among princes, nobles, officials, and those individuals who had performed some meritorious service. Besides its role in the framing of laws, the *Genroin* would have two specific powers: first, the prosecution of high government officials and second, the right of interpellation. The *Daigishiin,* on the other hand, would be a popularly elected chamber, the members of which would serve a four-year term with elections for half the total membership every two years. The draft constitution also contained a bill of rights for all Japanese subjects which guaranteed individual rights and freedoms, with one sweeping qualification: all rights and freedoms could be modified by law. Thus freedom of religion, the right of free assembly and association, the right of private secret communication, freedom from unlawful arrest and imprisonment, and the right to move about freely could be legislated out of existence.

The oligarchs did not react favorably to the draft constitution submitted by the *Genroin* committee. They opposed the provisions regarding the division of legislative power, particularly the clause regarding the budget and taxes.[29] Ito feared a parliamentary financial check on the powers of government and objected to parliamentary control of the annual budget and imperial expenditures, citing the historical example of the decline of the

---

29. Fujii, *Nihon kempo seitei shi,* 238.

The Democratic Movement, 1876-1881

power of the British crown. He was also apprehensive of the Emperor and parliament "sharing" equally the legislative power, which he regarded as a step in the direction of parliamentary supremacy.[30] Iwakura, who had only reluctantly accepted the decision to establish a constitution, was even more apprehensive. Since 1875, he had been worried over the possibility of parliamentary controls over imperial powers and so concerned was he with the work of the *Genroin* committee that, in March 1878, he had proposed that the *Dajokan* establish its own bureau to compile a constitution which would fortify the imperial powers.[31] Ito and Iwakura finally took the lead in suggesting that the draft be revised with the purpose of having it conform more closely to the traditional imperial system.[32] The *Genroin* committee then undertook to revise the draft, a task which was not completed until July 1880.

In December 1879, at the prompting of Iwakura, the Emperor asked the oligarchs to submit written opinions regarding the *Genroin* draft constitution, and each was asked to comment upon the advisability of establishing a constitution and a national parliament.[33] While the written opinions of the oligarchs differed in detail, all were united on two points. They agreed that the constitution should be established in the future, and that it should place sovereignty in the person of the Emperor. Moreover, they expressed the opinion that the government should take gradual

---

30. Suzuki Yasuzo, *Kempo no rekishiteki kenkyu* (Toyko, 1934), 162-163.
31. Miyakoshi, *Nihon kensei kiso shiryo*, 217-221; Osatake, *Nihon kensei shi taiko*, II, 464. Until 1873, Iwakura had been the link between the imperial court and the Satsuma-Choshu coalition led by Okubo, Saigo, and Kido. From 1873 on, he had given his full support to Okubo in the suppression of the samurai revolts and the democratic movement. Iwakura had come to represent an extreme point of view which sought to deny the public any channels for the expression of public opinion. Later in 1882, he went so far as to submit a proposal for the abolition of local assemblies. Osatake, *Nihon kensei shi taiko*, II, 482; Fujii, *Nihon kempo seitei shi*, 243-244.
32. Osatake, *Nihon kensei shi taiko*, II, 477-478. Both Ito and Iwakura clearly based their objections upon the fact that the draft constitution did not conform to *kokutai*. However, Ito and the oligarchs were extremely anxious to draft a constitution that would unite the various political factions solidly behind the government.
33. This order was addressed to the following oligarchs: Ito, Yamagata, Kuroda, Oki, Inouye, Yamada, and Okuma. All replied with the exception of Okuma, who did not answer until the spring of 1881, at which time he precipitated a crisis in the government over the issue of the constitution.

steps toward the establishment of a parliament. Each opinion began with an historical summary of the manner in which the program of gradual reform was currently being implemented, and each cited the imperial rescript of 1875 as the ultimate sanction for such a policy.[34]

Yamagata, who had reached the conclusion that the leaders of the democratic movement were only waiting for an opportune moment to overthrow the government,[35] had for several years advocated the establishment of a constitution and a parliament.[36] He expressed the view that the government was forced to decide on some general constitutional principles, and he suggested that the government submit those principles for discussion to a national conference of prefectural-assembly representatives. Such a body, he felt, could provide the nucleus around which a parliament could be established in the future.[37]

Inouye made several noteworthy suggestions. He proposed that the government first establish an upper house of ex-samurai and nobles, partly elected and partly appointed, that would counterbalance a popularly elected lower house; moreover, he advised that the upper house, not the lower, should have the ultimate power to pass judgment on taxes and the budget. Regarding the drafting of the constitution, he recommended that the task be delegated to the upper house acting in consultation with the *Dajokan*. Final approval would be the prerogative of the Emperor.[38]

Ito and Oki both cautioned against changing the system of government too hurriedly, and both regarded the demand for a parliament as a dangerous attack on the doctrine of imperial sovereignty. Like Inouye, they suggested the creation of an upper

---

34. The imperial rescript of April 14, 1875, which announced the plan for the reorganization of the government, proclaimed that "constitutional government would be established in gradual stages."
35. Osatake, *Nihon kensei shi taiko*, II, 521-522.
36. Tokutomi Iichiro, *Koshaku Yamagata Aritomo den* (Tokyo, 1939), II, 839.
37. Miyakoshi, *Nihon kensei kiso shiryo*, 274. Appendix IV of this study is a translation of Yamagato's opinion.
38. *Ibid.*, 291-292.

The Democratic Movement, 1876-1881

house of nobles as a bulwark of the government's power.[39] Kuroda, citing the examples of Prussian history, stressed the need for an extension of popular education before convoking a parliament, and he was more concerned to expand the nation's military power and industrial production.[40] Yamada warned that increased popular participation in government was inevitable, but he too suggested that the government continue to maintain the present assemblies, the *Genroin* and *Chihokankaigi,* so as to judge their results before taking any further action.[41]

In December 1880, the second completed draft of a constitution by the *Genroin* committee was reported to the throne by Oki, who had replaced Prince Arisugawa as President of the *Genroin.* It is interesting to note that the members of the *Genroin* were permitted to affix their private opinions. Most of them were enthusiastic supporters of the draft, which was almost an exact duplicate of the 1878 constitution that had been rejected by the oligarchs;[42] moreover, some called for complete cabinet responsibility to parliament.[43] The *Genroin* committee had evidently continued working for some sort of a compromise between the Japanese imperial system and parliamentary government, and the only significant changes from the 1878 draft were a modification of the wording regarding the division of legislative power between the Emperor and parliament and a clearer statement of the power of impeachment which would rest with both houses instead of only the

---

39. For Ito's opinion, see *ibid.,* 294-300; for Oki, *ibid.,* 301-310. In 1905, commenting on this period, Ito stated: "At that time we had not yet arrived at the stage of distinguishing clearly between political opposition on one hand, and treason to the established order of things on the other. The virtues necessary for the smooth working of any constitution, such as love of freedom of speech, love of publicity of proceedings, the spirit of tolerance for opinions opposed to one's own, etc., had yet to be learned by long experience." Ito, *loc. cit.,* 130. A translation of Ito's views is included in Appendix V hereto.
40. Miyakoshi, *Nihon kensei kiso shiryo,* 277-280.
41. *Ibid.,* 281-284.
42. For the text and explanation of this document, see Asai, *Genroin no kempo hensan temmatsu,* 161-174, 174-336. The explanation is a detailed commentary on measures in other constitutions that are similar to each article of the *Genroin* draft.
43. The attitude of Fukuoka Kotei with regard to this matter is noteworthy; he expressed a strong desire for parliamentary initiation of legislation and a cabinet system that would be responsible to parliament and not the Emperor. Osatake, *Nihon kensei shi taiko,* II, 481.

Genroin. This second draft constitution again omitted any definite statement regarding sovereignty, but the drafters seem to have implied that sovereignty was shared by the Emperor and parliament.

The second draft constitution was no more favorably received by the oligarchs than the first.[44] They still regarded it as a dangerous compromise with the theory of parliamentary supremacy. From the point of view of Ito and his followers, it would place serious restrictions upon the authority of the government; moreover, it did not provide for the financial independence of the government or for an imperial ordinance power. That these measures were important in their minds can be seen in the great care taken by the oligarchs to provide for them in the constitution which was ultimately established. Final action regarding the draft was taken by the oligarchs in March 1881, when it was officially rejected, and Oki and Yamada were ordered to revise it. At the same time, the *Genroin* committee was abolished.[45]

By the spring of 1881, the government had not yet found a satisfactory solution to the constitutional problem; however, among the oligarchs there was a general awareness of the necessity to establish a constitution and a parliament in order to meet the demands of the democratic movement. It is clear that limited concessions, such as politically ineffective local assemblies rationalized by the philosophy of gradual progress, were unacceptable to Itagaki and his followers. By 1881, the whole nation was in the grips of a great political debate, and the agitation against Satsuma-Choshu absolutism mounted. It is equally clear that the alternative policy of restricting political rights and liberties could not be maintained indefinitely. That the situation was indeed explosive can be judged by the political crisis that arose in the summer of 1881, when events related to Okuma's defection from the oligarchy finally forced the government to promise the establishment of a national parliament.

---

44. Iwakura remained the most apprehensive and again proposed that the *Dajokan* establish its own constitutional investigating bureau. *Ibid.,* 665.

45. Fujii and Moriya, *Sogo nihon shi taikei,* 238. Furthermore, Terajima Munenori from Satsuma became President of the *Genroin,* replacing a Hizen clansman.

Chapter V
The Constitutional Debate, 1881-1885

The late spring and summer of 1881 proved to be the decisive period with regard to the establishment of a constitution and the convocation of a parliament in Japan. The government's efforts at drawing up a constitution had been temporarily postponed when the oligarchs refused to approve the *Genroin's* revised draft constitution of December 1880. However, the democratic movement had reached such proportions that they[1] found it increasingly difficult to ignore the demand for a parliament. Moreover, by the spring of 1881, there were signs of a new split within the oligarchy as a result of the sudden shift toward liberalism by Okuma Shigenobu, who proposed the immediate establishment of parliamentary government. This development so weakened the solidarity of the oligarchs' position that, when they were faced with a serious domestic crisis in the summer of 1881 as a result of the Hokkaido properties scandal, they were no longer able to withstand popular demands for reform. Finally, in October, the Emperor promised the people a constitution and a parliament.

The discussion within the government of the draft constitution compiled by the *Genroin* committee had brought into the open a new split within the ruling oligarchy. In December 1879, when the Emperor had asked for written opinions from each of the oligarchs with regard to a constitution and a parliament, Okuma had refused to comply. When the *Sadaijin,* Prince Arisugawa, pressed him, Okuma replied that he desired to state his

---

1. The important posts in the government were filled as follows: Members of the *Dajokan* included the *Dajodaijin,* Sanjo Sanetomi; *Sadaijin,* Prince Arisugawa Taruhito; *Udaijin,* Iwakura Tomomi; Councillors *(Sangi),* Oki Takato (President of the *Genroin*), Okuma Shigenobu, Ito Hirobumi, Terajima Munemori, Inouye Kaoru (Minister of Foreign Affairs), Yamagata Aritomo (Chief of Staff of the Army), Kuroda Kiyotaka (Commissioner of Colonization and Development of Hokkaido), Saigo Tsugumichi, and Yamada Akiyoshi. The Ministry was completed as follows: Home Affairs, Matsukata; Finance, Sano; Navy, Enomoto; War, Oyama; Education, Kono; Public Works, Yamao, and Justice, Tanaka.

opinions in an imperial audience; moreover, he did not want them to become known to others.[2] His request was denied, but in March 1881 Okuma submitted to the Emperor a written report that had been prepared by two of his followers.[3] In this report, Okuma urged that the government establish a parliament immediately. He suggested that parliamentary representatives be elected by the end of 1882 and that parliament be convened early in 1883. He expressed the hope that "the leader of a party possessing a majority of seats in parliament should be entrusted with the conduct of public affairs, but he should retire when his party falls into a minority." He emphasized that "constitutional government is party government," and "when a party's program wins the support of the majority of the nation, that party should come into power."[4]

There is no clear explanation of the motives behind Okuma's sudden deviation. It seems that he regarded parliamentary government as a means of liquidating the Satsuma-Choshu oligarchy and personally assuming leadership in the government. Paramount perhaps was his ambition, and in this respect his stand was the culmination of a struggle for power between Ito and himself that had developed since the death of Okubo in 1878. Ito, who succeeded to Kido's leadership of the Choshu faction in the government, had been able to get along well with his Satsuma colleagues. On the other hand, Okuma, who had deliberately refrained from getting involved in the Satsuma-Choshu rivalry, slowly gained supporters among the more liberal-minded young college graduates who had entered government service. But while Okuma held an important position in the government and was supported by friends in responsible posts, his ambition was kept

---

2. Fujii and Moriya, *Sogo nihon shi taikei*, 248.
3. For the text of this document see Miyakoshi, *Nihon kensei kiso shiryo*, 311-323. The report was written by Ono Azusa, who had lived in England for three years, and Yano Fumio, who admitted he was influenced by British parliamentary practices. Osatake, *Nihon kensei shi taiko*, II, 567-568. An English version may be found in Appendix VI of the present study.
4. Miyakoshi, *Nihon kensei kiso shiryo*, 331-332.

The Constitutional Debate, 1881-1885

in check by the powerful forces of Satsuma and Choshu.[5] Thus it seems that Okuma was taking advantage of the increasing pressure put on the government by the democratic movement.[6]

Okuma's report was referred to the *Dajokan* by the Emperor in June, and Prince Arisugawa, not heeding a request by Okuma not to disclose its contents to the oligarchs or the *Daijin,* showed it in secret to Iwakura and Sanjo. Iwakura went directly to Okuma and discussed the obvious differences of opinion between Okuma and the other leaders of the government. Then, after consultation with Sanjo, Iwakura showed the report to Ito,[7] who was indignant, claiming that Okuma had given the Emperor advice that was not consistent with views that he had expressed earlier. Ito threatened to resign and refused to attend further sessions of the *Dajokan*.[8] Early in July, however, Iwakura arranged a temporary reconciliation between Ito and Okuma in order to

---

5. The Satsuma-Choshu oligarchy was well aware of the threat that Okuma presented. In February 1880, the *Dajokan* was reorganized and Okuma was ousted from his position as Minister of Finance. Fujii and Moriya, *Sogo nihon shi taikei,* 588. As early as 1869-1870 the samurai leaders of the Satsuma-Choshu faction in the central government recognized Okuma as a threat to their domination of the administration. When the Departments of Home Affairs and Finance were merged in September 1869, there was a brief struggle for power within the new department between Okuma and Ito, and when Okuma got the upper hand, he aroused the opposition of part of the Satsuma-Choshu faction, which feared that the power of this department would be equal to that of the *Dajokan* council. Okubo and his followers, who were the most disturbed, threatened to resign unless Okuma was stripped of his power; however, a solution was reached in 1870, when on August 6th, the department was divided into a separate Department of Finance and Department of Home Affairs. As a personal concession to Okuma, he was admitted to the *Dajokan* council on September 26, but his administrative duties were confined to the Department of Finance. *Ibid.,* 262-264. It is interesting to note that these two departments were temporarily merged for a second time in the government reorganization of 1871. Ijichi, commenting on the relationship between Okuma and the oligarchs, states: "The balance of power was a doctrine that governed the acts and thoughts of the rulers of the day. The two great parties of Satsuma and Choshu . . . were so jealous of their respective power that they would not tolerate anything tending to disturb the great principle of equilibrium. Hence the frequent attempts at the maintenance of an equal share of power between the two major parties." *The Life of Marquis Shigenobu Okuma* (Tokyo, 1940), 119-120.

6. Sir George Sansom comments: "Such being the case, this aspect of a struggle for parliament was in essence not a clear issue between conservatives and progressives, advocting Western principles of government, but rather the perpetuation of old rivalries in a modern setting." *The Western World and Japan,* 346.

7. Osatake, *Nihon kensei shi taiko,* II, 569-570.

8. Takahashi Shingo, "Meiji juyonen no seihen ni tsuite," *Waseda seiji keizaigaku zasshi,* LXI (1938), 19-21.

restore unity in the government, and Okuma withdrew his opinion.⁹

The constitutional issue, however, does not tell the whole story of the Ito-Okuma rivalry. In the spring of 1881, a difference arose between Okuma and the Satsuma-Choshu oligarchy concerning the government's deflationary economic policy. In the first few years of the Meiji era, the government had undertaken to develop the resources of Hokkaido and in 1869 established the Office of the Commissioner of Colonization and Development of Hokkaido and accorded the Commissioner, Kuroda Kiyotaka of Satsuma, ministerial rank. In 1871 the government approved a ten-year development program with a yearly expenditure of one million yen to encourage immigration and to institute public works projects in Hokkaido. In 1881, when the oligarchs adopted the general policy of transferring government-owned enterprises to private interests and decided to end the program in Hokkaido, Kuroda helped to organize a private company which offered to purchase the government-owned enterprises in Hokkaido for 380,000 yen to be paid over a thirty-year period without interest.¹⁰ This proposal was approved in secret by the *Dajokan* on July 28, but Okuma steadfastly opposed Kuroda's offer.¹¹ On August 1, the sale was officially confirmed when Sanjo, intimidated by Kuroda, obtained the approval of the Emperor, who had left Tokyo on a tour of northern Japan.¹²

News of the proposed transaction was disseminated widely after July 26, when the *Tokyo-Yokohama Mainichi* published an editorial attacking it. Popular indignation arose immediately, and the press including the pro-government *Tokyo Nichi Nichi* and the *Meiji Nippo,* was united in an indictment of the sale.¹³ When

---

9. Watanabe Ritsuzan, "Meiji juyonen seihen ni tsuite," *Meiji bunka kenkyu,* II (1934), 9; Nakamura Kikuo, *Nihon kindaika to Fukuzawa Yukichi* (Tokyo, 1950), 107.
10. Osatake, *Nihon kensei shi taiko,* II, 572-573.
11. As Nobutake Ike explains, Okuma's close connection with the Mitsubishi Company, which stood to lose certain navigation rights to Hokkaido if the government properties were sold, helps to explain his opposition to the sale. *The Beginnings of Political Democracy in Japan,* 98.
12. Watanabe, *loc. cit.,* 6.
13. Nakamura, *op. cit.,* 114-115.

THE CONSTITUTIONAL DEBATE, 1881-1885

the leaders of the democratic movement began to make use of the disclosure to denounce the "clan oligarchy," the incident soon reached the proportions of a national scandal. When it became evident that Okuma's followers, many of them Keio University graduates under the influence of the liberalism of Fukuzawa Yukichi, led the agitation for reform, the oligarchs thought that Okuma was directing the campaign in the hope of being carried to power on the crest of a wave of popular support.[14] Ito and the oligarchs suspected that Okuma's predilection for the democratic movement was based upon his personal ambition and a secret alliance with Fukuzawa and the Mitsubishi Company.[15]

It is clear that Okuma played no direct part in the popular attack upon the government since he was not in Tokyo, having accompanied the Emperor on his tour of the north; and it does not seem that he sent any instructions to his friends.[16] However, various rumors involving Okuma, Fukuzawa, and the Mitsubishi Company, which contained threats to the Satsuma-Choshu clique, were taken seriously by the oligarchs.[17] Ito acted to cancel the inopportune Hokkaido transaction, to dismiss Okuma from the *Dajokan,* and to issue an imperial rescript proclaiming the establishment of a national parliament. Ito wanted to have the concurrence of Iwakura, who had gone to Kyoto, and had Sanjo send a letter on September 6 asking him to return to the capital.[18] It

---

14. *Ibid.,* 115-116.
15. For evidence of Ito's judgment of Okuma, Osatake cites an entry in the diary of Sasaki Takayuki: "According to a confidential talk I had with Ito, Okuma personally favors the democratic movement. He feels that there is no hope for the government and has secretly joined forces . . . with Fukuzawa Yukichi and the Mitsubishi Company." Osatake, *Nihon kensei shi taiko,* II, 576.
16. Ijichi, *op. cit.,* 576.
17. There is much evidence of a circumstantial nature to justify the fears of the oligarchs. For example, there was a close economic relationship between Okuma, the Mitsubishi Company, and Fukuzawa Yukichi, as well as their common support of laissez-faire economic principles. Ike, *Political Democracy,* 97-98. For specific details of the various rumors that were circulating, see Osatake, *Nihon kensei shi taiko,* II, 575-581. The relationship between Okuma and Fukuzawa was regarded as particularly dangerous, since it was well known that Fukuzawa supported the adoption of parliamentary government, and as a matter of fact, he was encouraging his students to prepare a written constitution based upon the English parliamentary system. Ijichi, *op. cit.,* 209-210. For a summary of Fukuzawa's activities in this period, see Nakamura, *op. cit.,* 128-136. For a denial of any plot by Okuma and Fukuzawa, see Watanabe, *loc. cit.,* 11-14.
18. Otsu Junichiro, *Dai nihon kensei shi* (Tokyo, 1929), II, 448.

seems, however, that Iwakura was not anxious to take immediate action on these matters, and he made no effort to leave.[19] Finally, after several pleas by Ito, Iwakura complied.[20] On his arrival in Tokyo on October 6, he conferred with Sanjo, and the two agreed to support the cancellation of the Hokkaido transaction and an announcement calling for the convocation of a national parliament; however, they reached no agreement with regard to Okuma. On the following day, Ito persuaded Iwakura to approve Okuma's ouster.[21]

On October 11, the Emperor and Okuma returned from northern Japan, and that very evening the members of the *Dajokan* met without Okuma.[22] They agreed to the cancellation of the Hokkaido sale and to the dismissal of Okuma. Their discussion and decision on the matter of a constitution and a parliament was based upon a group of principles that Iwakura had submitted earlier as a refutation of Okuma's written opinion.[23]

In July, Iwakura, who had finally come to concede the inevitability of a parliament, had presented a summary of his views to Sanjo and Prince Arisugawa for the Emperor's consideration in which he outlined what he regarded as an acceptable constitutional system for Japan.[24] Iwakura proposed that the *Dajokan* establish its own committee to draft a constitution. This committee, which would include only the *Daijin* and three or four Coun-

---

19. Watanabe, *loc. cit.*, 15. Ike suggests: "It may be that he did not wish to see the Sat-Cho faction strengthened. In any case he was not anxious to see Okuma forced out of the [*Dajokan*]." *Political Democracy*, 98. This view is supported by Otsu, *Dai nihon kensei shi*, II, 448-449.
20. For a summary of the government's efforts, see Otsu, *Dai nihon kensei shi*, II, 449-451.
21. *Ibid.*, 452.
22. Fujii, *Nihon kempo seitei shi*, 258-259. Present at the meeting were Sanjo, Prince Arisugawa, Iwakura, Terajima, Yamagata, Ito, Kuroda, Saigo, Inouye, and Yamada.
23. Osatake, *Nihon kensei shi taiko*, II, 599.
24. The following discussion of Iwakura's opinion is based upon the text of his suggestions which is included in Miyakoshi, *Nihon kensei kiso shiryo*, 324-337, and Otsu, *Dai nihon kensei shi*, II, 411-419, 788-796. Iwakura's opinion was drafted by Inouye Kowashi, a young bureaucrat who had come under the influence of the German professor of jurisprudence, Hermann Roessler. Osatake, *Nihon kensei shi taiko*, II, 592. Roessler, a protégé of Rudolph Gneist, was an authority on English and German constitutional law. He had arrived in Japan in 1878, and for the next decade served as an adviser to the Japanese government. For a sketch of the influence of Roessler in this period see Suzuki Yasuzo, "Nihon kempo seitei ni Hermann Roessler no kiyo" in *Nihon kempo shi kenkyu* (Tokyo, 1935), 125-169. A translation of Iwakura's opinion is included as Appendix VII.

cillors of State, would work in secret and submit a draft to the *Dajokan* for its approval. As a guide for the committee, Iwakura appended the following fundamental principles:

1. The Constitution shall emanate from the Emperor and the policy of a gradual approach toward constitutional government shall prevail.
2. The Emperor shall have supreme command over the army and navy, declare war, make peace, conclude treaties, etc.; moreover, the Emperor will direct the national administration.
3. The organization of the cabinet shall not be subjected to the intervention of parliament. Except for those administrative affairs that are of fundamental importance to the state, for which all ministers shall be jointly responsible, each minister shall only be individually responsible for administrative affairs under his official jurisdiction. Ministers shall be responsible to the Emperor and not to parliament.
4. Parliament shall consist of two houses: an upper house composed of members appointed by the Emperor and members elected from among the ranks of peers and former samurai, and a lower house of popularly elected representatives.
5. The election law for the lower house shall include a property qualification for the suffrage, while the electors for the peerage and ex-samurai shall not be subjected to property qualifications.
6. All legislative bills shall be initiated by the government.
7. When parliament does not pass an annual budget bill, the government may execute the provisions of the budget of the previous year.[25]
8. With regard to the rights of citizens, constitutional provisions of other nations shall be consulted.

Iwakura also expressed his views on the adaptability of foreign systems of government. He felt that the British system of parliamentary government was not suited to Japan's needs because it was not compatible with the institution of the Emperor, and he cited the fact that the British king had lost his power to parliament and had become a mere figurehead.[26] On the other hand, Iwakura looked with favor upon the Prussian system in which the king remained the center of power. He was particularly impressed by the fact that the Prussian king selected his own cabinet, which remained responsible to him. In general, Iwakura was seeking

---

25. According to Inouye Kowashi, this provision was derived from the Spanish Constitution of 1845 and article 109 of the Prussian Constitution of 1850. Ito Hirobumi (ed.), *Kempo shiryo* (Tokyo, 1934), I, 630.
26. Miyakoshi, *Nihon kensei kiso shiryo*, 329-330.

additional sanctions for a highly centralized authoritarian government.[27]

The members of the *Dajokan,* who had been thinking along similar lines, accepted Iwakura's thesis that they might be able to adapt Prussian ideas and institutions to the special needs and conditions of Japan. With regard to a parliament, they suggested to the Emperor that a bicameral body be established; however, they emphasized that the government should not proceed too hastily and that the parliament should not seriously restrict the powers of the Emperor.[28]

When this evening meeting of the *Dajokan* broke up, Ito and Saigo called on Okuma at midnight and asked him to resign. On the following day, Okuma and many of his followers tendered their resignations;[29] the government announced that the sale of the properties in Hokkaido was cancelled.[30] The climax of this dramatic series of events was reached when the *Dajodaijin,* Sanjo Sanetomi, promulgated an imperial rescript in which the government promised to establish a parliament in 1890; however, the rescript threatened reprisals against agitation for immediate action.[31] This commitment to convoke a parliament was an important victory for the democratic movement; however, by its terms, the oligarchs secured a free hand until 1890, a period in which they hoped to consolidate their positions and power. Actually, the extensive activities of the democratic movement in the summer of 1881 tended to cement the bond between Satsuma and Choshu statesmen, who undertook jointly to prepare for the

---

27. *Ibid.,* 333-338.
28. *Ibid.,* 339-343.
29. A list of those who resigned includes Yano Fumio, Ozaki Yukio, Inukai Tsuyoshi, and Ono Azusa. For the names of others, see Fujii, *Nihon kempo seitei shi,* 261, and Osatake, *Nihon kensei shi taiko,* II, 590-591. It is interesting to note that even before Okuma's resignation, the government had completed a list of those who were to be dismissed from service for being his supporters.
30. Osatake, *Nihon kensei shi taiko,* II, 588. Kuroda's indiscretion was not taken seriously, and he remained in his post as Councillor.
31. McLaren, *Japanese Government Documents,* 86-87. For the full text, see Appendix VIII of this study.

opening of parliament and to prevent, if possible, the rise of a strong opposition among the people.[32]

The imperial rescript of October 12 did not silence the democratic movement. On the contrary, it encouraged the formation of political parties which put forward their own platforms regarding the nature of the proposed constitution and parliament. The most important of these parties was the *Jiyuto* (Liberal Party), which had been organized in November 1880 by some members of the defunct *Aikokusha*. This group, led by Ueki Emori and Kono Hironaka, felt that only through continuous pressure could the government be forced to approve a constitution that included institutional checks upon the oligarchy.[33] In 1881 an enlarged *Jiyuto* was organized with a national network of rural parties that sent representatives to an annual convention in Tokyo. An election of party officers was held on October 30, 1881, and Itagaki was elected President and Nakayama Nobuyuki, Vice-President. At the same time, the *Jiyuto* adopted a democratic platform based upon the party's goal of responsible parliamentary government. On the whole, the *Jiyuto* was the most democratic of the political parties in that its political philosophy was based upon the principle of popular sovereignty; its leaders campaigned on the premise that the country existed chiefly for the people and not for the sovereign or an oligarchy.

It was not until the spring of 1882 that another national political party was organized. On March 15, a group of disgruntled former bureaucrats[34] led by Okuma joined with intellectuals from Keio University to form the *Rikken Kaishinto* (Constitutional

---

32. Shortly thereafter the personnel of the government was reorganized as follows: Councillors, Ito, Inouye (Minister of Foreign Affairs), Yamagata, Kuroda, Kawamura (Minister of Navy), Matsukata (Minister of Finance), Fukuoka (Minister of Education), Oki (Minister of Public Works, Minister of Justice). Saigo was Minister of Agriculture and Commerce; Yamada, Minister of Home Affairs; Terajima, President of the *Genroin;* Oyama, Minister of War. Fujii, *Nihon kempo seitei shi,* 261.

33. For the formation and nature of the *Jiyuto,* see Ike, *Political Democracy,* 101-104, 148.

34. Among this group were Kono Toshikama, Maejima Hisoka, Kitabatake Harufusa, Yano Fumio, Ozaki Yukio, and Inukai Tsuyoshi, all of whom had resigned from the government when Okuma was dismissed from office.

The Making of the Meiji Constitution

Reform Party).³⁵ The *Kaishinto*, supported by wealthy merchants and industrialists like the Mitsubishi Company and guided by the ideals of Fukuzawa Yukichi, formulated a more moderate political program than that of the *Jiyuto*. The platform of the *Kaishinto* placed sovereignty in the legislature, since that body represented both the sovereign and the people.³⁶ Its leaders felt that monarchical absolutism would disappear with the establishment of the constitutional government, and that hence the sovereignty of the state should reside in the parliament, as it did in England. The *Kaishinto*, through its press organs, the *Tokyo-Yokohama Mainichi* and the *Yubin Hochi*, also urged that the constitution be drafted by a national convention as a symbol of the termination of authoritarianism.³⁷

In an attempt to counterbalance the formation of the *Jiyuto* and *Kaishinto*, both of which were actively stirring up interest in political and economic questions, the oligarchs set about sponsoring a political party that represented their views. On March 18 and 19, 1882, the *Rikken Teiseito* (Constitutional Imperial Party) was organized by Fukuchi Genichiro, Maruyama Sakura, Mizuno Torajiro, Tani Tateki, Sasaki Takayuki, and Okamoto Takeo. Fukuchi, owner of the pro-government *Tokyo Nichi Nichi*, had been a close friend of Kido Koin and, after Kido's death, he

---

35. The *Kaishinto* soon had numerous affiliates. Osatake, *Nihon kensei shi taiko*, II, 636-637. The newspaper *Choya* claimed that there were 183 parties in October 1882, of which fifty-nine were affiliated with the *Jiyuto* and forty-two with the *Kaishinto*.
36. The platform of the *Kaishinto* also contained the following provisions:
   1. Preserve the dignity of the imperial house and promote the happiness of the people.
   2. Internal reform shall precede the extension of national rights and prestige.
   3. Establish local self-government by restricting the sphere of interference by the central government.
   4. Extend universal suffrage gradually.
   The business interests of the *Kaishinto* are clearly revealed in the following two provisions:
   5. Avoid complications with foreign nations in order to promote commercial intercourse.
   6. Reform the monetary system on the principle of a "hard money" system.
Both the government and business interests desired to end the inflationary trend in the economy which was having harmful effects upon the development of industry and stability of foreign trade. For a discussion of this, see Ike, *Political Democracy*, 139-140. The complete platform of the *Kaishinto* is included in Miyakoshi, *Nihon kensei kiso shiryo*, 404-405.
37. Osatake, *Nihon kensei shi taiko*, II, 596.

THE CONSTITUTIONAL DEBATE, 1881-1885

allied with the Choshu faction led by Ito and Inouye. Together with Okamoto, manager of the *Tokyo Nichi Nichi,* he planned the formation of a conservative political party. Fukuchi joined forces with Maruyama, who was associated with Yamada, and with Mizuno, owner of the *Toyo Shimpo,* which vigorously opposed the democratic movement.[38]

Whereas the *Jiyuto* and *Kaishinto* drew their members largely from intellectuals, rural landlord-industrialists, the urban middle class, and peasants, the membership of the *Teiseito* was generally confined to persons and groups that were connected with the government. The *Teiseito* drew upon the ranks of rising young bureaucrats, including the officials of prefectural and local government, Shinto and Buddhist priests, public school teachers, and businessmen closely connected with the government. It also had the active support of such high government officials as Ito, Inouye, and Yamada;[39] moreover, in the field of publicity, it was championed by the *Tokyo Nichi Nichi, Meiji Nippo,* and *Toyo Shimpo,* all of which campaigned to defend the government and to make the opposition parties appear treasonable.[40]

While the *Teiseito* did not gain a mass following,[41] it was important as an instrument for the popularization of the political views and objectives of the ruling oligarchy. The party's political program was drafted by Fukuchi and approved in a private conference with Ito, Inouye, and Yamada.[42] This platform, which argued emphatically that sovereignty rested in the Emperor, stated:[43]

---

38. Otsu, *Dai nihon kensei shi,* II, 556-568. These three men were closely allied with the government. Besides the *Tokyo Nichi Nichi,* which was called the "semi-official gazette," the government employed Maruyama to publish the *Meiji Nippo* and Mizuno to issue the *Toyo Shimpo;* all these preached the German doctrine of state autocracy to combat the principle of popular rights and freedoms. As a result of the influence of Fukuchi, Maruyama, and Mizuno, the party began to be called the *sanninto* or the "three-man party." Osatake, *Nihon kensei shi taiko,* II, 633.

39. Otsu, *Dai nihon kensei shi,* II, 549; Mivakoshi, *Nihon kensei kiso shiryo,* 459.

40. For a summary of the editorial conflicts between the press in this period, see Osatake, *Nihon kensei shi taiko,* II, 597-603.

41. On October 13 and 14, 1882, the *Teiseito* convened a conference in Tokyo which was attended by only two hundred people. For this and other unsuccessful attempts to gain popular support, see Otsu, *Dai nihon kensei shi,* II, 558-559.

42. *Ibid.,* 550.

43. This political program, which was originally published in the *Tokyo Nichi Nichi* on March 18, 1882, is included in Osatake, *Nihon kensei shi taiko,* II, 633-634.

The Making of the Meiji Constitution

1. We pledge ourselves to support the Imperial Decree of October 12, 1881, which fixes the date of the convocation of a parliament for 1890, and to refrain absolutely from any discussion of its alteration.

2. We pledge ourselves to abide by the constitution to be granted by the Emperor, as proclaimed in the said Imperial Decree.

3. We maintain that it is indisputable that the sovereignty of the Empire resides in the Emperor, and that the exercises of certain powers of the parliament should be regulated by the constitution.

4. We believe that the legislature must be a two-chamber system.

5. We also believe that it is necessary to restrict the electorate by some system of qualification.

6. We maintain that the parliament should be given the power of enacting laws concerning the internal affairs of state.

7. We believe that it is necessary that an absolute veto power over all legislation should be left in the hands of the Emperor.

8. We maintain that the holders of all judicial offices should be made independent of the executive with the complete development of the judicial system.

9. We maintain that naval and military men should be excluded from the politics of the country.

10. We maintain that freedom of meetings, associations, and public speech should be restricted only in reference to the disturbances of the public peace.

Confronted by two powerful opposition parties which continued to gain strength, the oligarchs felt that it was necessary to take stronger measures to counter their influence and relied upon a policy of suppression. In June 1882, the government issued a revised ordinance regarding public meetings and associations in a determined attempt to ban political organizations, public meetings, and political discussions that were critical of its leadership or its policies;[44] moreover, the Home Minister and the police were directed to observe and disband any meeting when they deemed it necessary for the "preservation of public peace and order." Local police and the chief of the Tokyo police were given the power to prohibit the speaker of a dissolved meeting from publicly discussing politics in their area of jurisdiction or anywhere in Japan for a period of not longer than one year; moreover, they were authorized to disband the political association or party involved if neces-

---

44. McLaren, *Japanese Government Documents*, 499-501.

The Constitutional Debate, 1881-1885

sary. Political associations were required to report to the police their constitutions, by-laws, and the names of all their members and to notify the police of every new entry and resignation; if an association desired to hold a meeting for the study, debate, or discussion of political topics, it was required to secure permission from the police three days in advance. These associations were also forbidden to advertise the nature of political meetings, to excite the public by agents or circulars, or to correspond or join with similar groups.[45] If these orders were violated, the offenders were liable to a fine or minor prison sentence. In April 1883, the Press Law of 1875 was also revised to place harsher restrictions upon the activities of opposition newspapers, particularly the highly critical *Jiyu* of the *Jiyuto* and the *Yubin Hochi* of the *Kaishinto*.[46]

The oligarchs also enacted measures to increase the efficiency of the national police system. In January 1881, the government carried out a minor reorganization of the police which more closely defined the control of the Home Minister directly over the Tokyo police and indirectly over the local police through the prefectural governors and the prefectural office of the *Keibucho* (High Constable).[47] In May 1886, the police system was again modified with a view to further centralization. Subject to the direction of the Prime Minister and the various ministries, the chief of the Tokyo Metropolitan Police took charge of national police affairs.[48] In this same period, the government organized a military police system within the army; at first established in Tokyo only, it soon spread to army divisional headquarters throughout Japan. In 1882, the Emperor issued a personal warning to the members

---

45. This last provision was designed to prevent the union of the *Jiyuto* and *Kaishinto*.
46. In 1883, the publication of forty-nine newspapers was suspended. The government continued to pursue a policy of oppression for some time; however, in December 1887, a revised press law was issued, considerably modifying the strict control of the press. The new law was drafted on the constitutional principle of "freedom of the press" which was shortly to be recognized in a limited fashion by the constitution of 1889. Under the new law, a prospective publisher only had to notify the authorities of his intention to publish a newspaper. The prefectural governor was stripped of his power to suppress newspapers or to confiscate the plant. Only the Home Minister retained such power.
47. McLaren, *Japanese Government Documents*, 299-301.
48. *Ibid.*, 312-313.

of the armed forces against possible involvement in political strife.[49]

The oligarchs also successfully interfered in the activities of the two major opposition parties in order to prevent the formation of a united opposition. In 1882, Ito and Inouye lured Itagaki and Goto from the *Jiyuto* by holding out the prize of a trip through Europe. In April 1882, Inouye had tried to get funds for the trip from Iwasaki of the Mitsubishi Company but failed; however, he was successful when he approached the rival Mitsui Company, which was rewarded by an extension to 1883 of an important contract with the army. In May, this action was approved by Ito, Iwakura, Matsukata, Yamada, and Saigo; then, Itagaki and Goto were approached in secret.[50] In July, Itagaki revealed to his friends that he was contemplating a trip to Europe on the pretext that it was not wise to leave the study of constitutional problems to the government alone. Finally, in November 1882, Itagaki and Goto departed from Japan and remained abroad until June 1883. There were important repercussions within the *Jiyuto*. Oishi Masami, Baba Tatsui, and Suehiro Tetcho took the lead in condemning the trip, and there was general suspicion regarding the source of the funds. When Itagaki refused to alter his plans, the three resigned from the party.

More important than this split within the leadership of the *Jiyuto* was the precipitation of a heated controversy between the *Jiyuto* and the *Kaishinto*. When knowledge of Itagaki's and Goto's trip leaked out, the *Tokyo-Yokohama Mainichi,* an important *Kaishinto* newspaper, published an editorial criticizing them and intimating that the government was financing the trip. This proved to be the signal for the beginning of a heated argument between the two parties. The *Jiyuto* denied the charges and used its own press organs to retaliate by attacking the *Kaishinto* as the tool of the Mitsubishi Company and labeling it as a profit-

---

49. Fujii Shinichi, *Tenno Seiji,* English edition (Tokyo, 1944), 348-349.
50. For a discussion of these events, see Osatake Takeki, "Itagaki Taisuke no seiko mondai," *Meiji seiji shi tembyo* (Tokyo, 1938), 151-179, or Osatake Takeki, "Seito shi no issetsu," *Meiji bunka kenkyu,* II, 27-46.

The Constitutional Debate, 1881-1885

making organization parading as a political party.[51] The net effect of these charges and countercharges was to widen the existing differences between the two parties and their leaders. Whatever basis there had been for a common front against the government was irretrievably lost; moreover, both parties were seriously harmed by the fact that they were discredited in the eyes of the general public. Thus the government's attempts to undermine the development of opposition political parties was successful. Constant suppression placed the parties at an unfair disadvantage, and clever meddling prevented the development of any coöperation between them.

The *Jiyuto* was also weakened by economic developments which eventually caused the party to split and disintegrate. After 1881, the coalition of interests in the party was given a severe test. In that year, the government's deflationary economic policy caused a general depression. Farm incomes dropped, and so long as land taxation remained high, there was an increasing tendency for the peasantry to be dispossessed of its land. As a result, coöperation between the peasantry and the local landlords broke down as peasant groups began to form radical political organizations which campaigned for lower taxes and interest rates. Cleavages developed in the *Jiyuto* when many of the local peasant associations came under the leadership of a radical wing in the *Jiyuto*, which began to advocate social and economic reform as well as political changes. The leaders of the *Jiyuto* tried to harmonize these differences in the winter of 1883-1884, but it was impossible to impose party discipline on the peasantry so long as the

---

51. Ike points out that the anti-Mitsubishi movement was instrumental in stirring up those *Jiyuto* members who were rural producers suffering under the marketing operations and high transport rates charged by the Mitsubishi Company. The attack on the Mitsubishi Company had the effect of serving the interests of the Mitsui Company, which was financing Itagaki's and Goto's trip. In 1882, the government, which had been convinced for some time that the Mitsubishi Company was providing Okuma with funds to carry on his political activities, had organized with the Mitsui Company a quasi-governmental Mutual Transportation Company *(Kyodo Unyu Kaisha)* to compete against the Mitsubishi Company. Ike also suggests that the *Jiyuto* campaign against the *Kaishinto* and Mitsubishi interests might be attributed to the fact that Komuro Nobuo, one of the founders of the new shipping company, was a friend of Furuzawa Uro, editor of the newspaper *Jiyu*. *Political Democracy*, 154-155.

demand for social and economic reform continued to grow. Finally on October 29, 1884, the *Jiyuto* was dissolved;[52] immediately thereafter, scattered peasant uprisings erupted throughout Japan.[53]

The *Kaishinto* did not dissolve itself as the *Jiyuto* had, but became a virtual nonentity in December 1884, when, after a disagreement among its leaders on economic policy, Okuma and Vice-President Kono Toshikama resigned, leaving Numa Morikazu and Ozaki Yukio to carry on as best they could.[54] Prior to these events, the government-supported *Teiseito* had been dissolved.

By 1885 the democratic movement was effectively checked by the government; while the democratic movement was not completely destroyed, it never again regained the effectiveness which it had displayed in 1880 and 1881. The oligarchs, on the other hand, were able to enact administrative reforms and draft a constitution in preparation for the first session of parliament in 1890.

---

52. Miyakoshi, *Nihon kensei kiso shiryo*, 462-467.
53. For a discussion of these revolts which sheds light on the division in the *Jiyuto*, see Ike, *Political Democracy*, 160-168.
54. Otsu, *Dai nihon kensei shi*, II, 697-700.

Chapter VI
Drafting the Meiji Constitution, 1881-1889

While the imperial rescript of October 12, 1881, and the subsequent formation of political parties precipitated a national debate regarding the nature of the proposed constitution and parliament, the oligarchs quietly began to implement measures to reorganize the structure of the government and to draft a constitution which would safeguard their political power. It is clear from their approval of Iwakura's theses that Ito and his colleagues were united upon principles of authoritarian government in which the Emperor would continue to serve as the source of their political power; however, they were confronted with the serious problem of fitting him into a constitutional structure that would place specific checks upon any democratic tendencies. Almost immediately after the promulgation of the October 12 rescript, the government turned its attention to this important question.

On October 21, a special bureau *(Sanjiin)* was established in the *Dajokan* to assist in drafting laws and regulations, managing the affairs of the various departments, and supervising the deliberations of the *Genroin;* but more important, it was to act as a consultative committee on laws pertaining to the establishment of the constitution.[1] Ito was selected as chairman of the *Sanjiin* with Tanaka Fujimaro as his deputy; its members included Saionji Kimmochi, Inouye Kowashi, Ito Myoji, Hirata Tosuke, and Kiyoura Keigo.[2]

Shortly thereafter, on February 3, 1882, the Emperor asked the three *Daijin* for advice concerning the implementation of the

---
1. McLaren, *Japanese Government Documents,* 82-86. This new body replaced the *Dajokan* committee system that has been established in March 1880. Under the committee system, the *Dajokan* had been divided into six sections, each of which exercised supervisory control over one or more of the administrative departments. *Ibid.,* 53-55, 96n. The *Sanjiin* functioned until the establishment of the cabinet in December 1885. *Ibid.,* 82n.

2. Osatake, *Nihon kensei shi taiko,* II, 655.

THE MAKING OF THE MEIJI CONSTITUTION

rescript of October 12.[3] In their reply on February 24, Sanjo, Prince Arisugawa, and Iwakura suggested that Ito be dispatched to Europe to study the operation of various systems of constitutional government. They also recommended that the constitution confer broad executive and legislative powers on the Emperor and guarantee the financial independence of the government and the imperial family; moreover, they urged that a system of nobility be created to form the basis for membership in the upper house of parliament.[4]

On March 3, the Emperor ordered Ito to lead a mission of investigation to Europe to study and observe various systems of government in operation.[5] As a guide for Ito's use, the rescript included a detailed list of questions regarding the political power and financial independence of the Emperor and his ministers.[6] Ito recruited a committee of nine assistants,[7] and on March 14, the group embarked from Yokohama. When they arrived in Europe, Ito dispatched Saionji and several others to Paris to study the constitution of the Third Republic. The remainder of the mission proceeded to Berlin. From May 27 to July 29, Ito, Ito Myoji, and Aoki Shuzo, Minister to Germany, attended a series of lectures by Rudolph Gneist, the well-known legal authority.

---

3. *Ibid.*, 655.

4. Miyakoshi, *Nihon kensei kiso shiryo*, 346-350.

5. *Ibid.*, 352-355. Shortly thereafter, the Emperor had Sanjo ask the *Dajokan* for a report regarding the preparations for the establishment of the constitution and parliament. *Ibid.*, 369. The reply of the *Dajokan* was nothing more than a general promise to do its utmost at home and abroad. *Ibid.*, 369-370.

6. As Sansom points out, "The government was interested in examining the practical working of systems of government in use in the West in order to ascertain what was most appropriate to the needs of Japan. Ito was not going to be guided by theory, but by personal observations and discussions with men of experience." Sansom, *The Western World and Japan*, 362. It is interesting to note that there is a great deal of speculation among historians regarding the authorship of the questions presented to Ito for his guidance; however, the most generally held opinion is that they were written by Inouye Kowashi under Iwakura's order. Fujii, *Nihon kempo seitei shi*, 286-289, and Osatake, *Nihon kensei shi taiko*, II, 662-664.

7. Ito's assistants included Saionji, Ito Myoji, and Hirata. According to Kaneko Kentaro, the membership of this group represented a compromise reached by the oligarchs to prevent domination by Choshu interests. For example, it is well known that Ito had desired to include Inouye Kowashi, but the *Dajokan* refused. Suzuki, *Nihon kensei shi gaisetsu*, 333.

Drafting the Constitution, 1881-1889

Aoki acted as interpreter for Ito while Ito Myoji took notes on the lectures in Japanese.[8]

Gneist's lectures reinforced Ito's convictions. Gneist based his lectures on the general principle that constitutions should be firmly rooted in national history. He compared the history of Japan with that of Prussia, and urged Ito to adopt a Prussian-style constitution. Most of Gneist's suggestions limited the power of parliament; he stressed the need to protect the supreme powers of the Emperor as exercised by his ministers. Specifically, he emphasized that ultimate control of foreign affairs, military matters, and legislation be entrusted to the Emperor.[9] With regard to the decisive matter of finance, Gneist pointed to the decline of the British crown and recommended a provision which had been inserted into the Prussian Constitution whereby the government was assured of the previous year's budget should parliament refuse or be unable to pass an appropriations bill.[10] He also told Ito to be certain that the financial resources of the imperial family were in no way controlled by parliament. Finally, he cautioned his listeners against calling a constitutional convention and advised that they establish a property qualification to limit suffrage.[11]

From Berlin, Ito and his party journeyed to Vienna, where Ito attended lectures by the famous jurist Lorenz von Stein. Stein lectured in English with Ito Myoji taking notes in the same language. After the notes were checked by Stein, Ito Myoji translated them into Japanese for Ito's benefit.[12] In his lectures, Stein outlined an authoritarian system of government called "bureaucratic constitutionalism," in which the state and the monarch

---

8. The following discussion is based upon Ito Myoji's notes in *Meiji bunka zenshu*, IV, 429-477, and a convenient summary of the notes in Suzuki Yasuzo, *Kempo no rekishiteki kenkyu* (Tokyo, 1933), 364-370.
9. *Meiji bunka zenshu*, IV, 432-436.
10. *Ibid.*, 451.
11. During this same period, Ito also attended daily lectures by Albert Mosse, a disciple of Gneist. Mosse's lectures, which were designed to supplement those of Gneist, also emphasized the necessity for making the Emperor the core of power in the government. For notes on these lectures, see Kiyomizu Shin, *Dokuo ni okeru Ito Hirobumi no torishirabe to nihon kempo* (Tokyo, 1939), 337-392.
12. *Ibid.*, 19-20. For notes of Stein's lectures, see *Meiji bunka zenshu*, IV, 498-613. For a summary of the lectures and a list of the lecture topics, see Osatake, *Nihon kensei shi taiko*, II, 707-711.

were synonymous. Opposed to universal suffrage and party government, Stein urged Ito to establish constitutional government not with cabinet responsibility to parliament but with paramount power in the hands of the ministers as representatives of the sovereign Emperor.[13] With regard to legislation, he advised that only the government should have the right to initiate bills and that the Emperor should have the absolute right to veto legislation.[14] Finally, he suggested that the management of the Imperial Household should be kept separate from the regular administration.[15]

It is difficult to estimate what Ito learned from his nine months of study under Gneist, Stein, and Mosse;[16] however, it is certain that his authoritarian opinions were more strongly confirmed. Remarks in his letters to Iwakura are perhaps the best indication of this.[17] Ito undoubtedly gained a broader general understanding of government, and it is evident that his study and observation reinforced his prejudice against democratic government and inclined him towards the adoption of a Prussian-style constitution.[18]

---

13. Kiyomizu, *op. cit.*, 243-245.
14. *Ibid.*, 255.
15. *Ibid.*, 319-320. It is interesting to note that Stein justified authoritarian government by a theory of society which he felt was applicable to both Germany and Japan. Stein, who equated the state with the person of the Emperor, was convinced that the chief purpose of the state was to resolve the clashing interests of society that resulted from the nineteenth century victory of industrialism over feudalism. According to Stein, the social tensions that accompanied this victory would disappear only through reforms carried out by the government. Norman feels that this concept appealed greatly to Ito, who hoped that the Japanese would accept a paternal government in the name of the Emperor. *Feudal Background of Japanese Politics*, 91.
16. After attending Stein's lectures at Vienna, Ito returned to Berlin, where he heard additional lectures by Mosse from November 14 to mid-December. After a Christmas vacation, Ito studied with Mosse from January 30 to February 9. Mosse later served in Japan from 1886-1890 as an adviser on local government. For notes on these additional lectures by Mosse, see Kiyomizu, *op. cit.*, 392-442.
17. Ito wrote to Iwakura: "I have been able to get a general understanding of the structure of the state. Later, I shall discuss with you how we can achieve the great objective of establishing imperial authority. Indeed, the tendency of our country today is to erroneously believe in the works of British, French, and American liberals and radicals as if they were Golden Rules, and thereby lead virtually to the overthrow of the State. In having found principles and means of combatting this trend, I believe I have rendered an important service to my country, and I feel inwardly that I can die a happy man." Quoted in Asai, *Meiji rikken shiso ni okeru eikoku gikai seido no eikyo*, 407. The translation is from Ike, *Political Democracy*, 175-176.
18. Miyakoshi, *Nihon kensei kiso shiryo*, 356-358; Osatake, *Nihon kensei shi taiko*, II, 675-676.

Drafting the Constitution, 1881-1889

Finally, when Ito actually undertook to compile a constitution, he did follow the advice of Stein to create a text that was simple, broad, and free from statements of theory.[19]

Ito and his party did not return directly to Japan. They stopped off at Paris, where Ito met Clemenceau; and they visited England, where Ito heard Herbert Spencer lecture on the theory of representative government.[20] From London, the mission embarked for Japan and arrived home in early August. Their homecoming was marked by a note of sadness, for on July 20 Iwakura had died.[21]

On March 17, the government established the *Seido Torishirabe Kyoku* (Bureau for the Investigation of Constitutional Systems) in the Imperial Household Department to undertake the drafting of the constitution. While the *Genroin* was the properly constituted body for such a task, it seems clear that the oligarchs desired to shield the work of drafting the constitution from any contact with public opinion. As part of the Imperial Household Department, the *Seido Torishirabe Kyoku* could work in secret with virtual immunity from outside criticism and at the same time create the illusion that the drafting was being done under the personal supervision of the Emperor.[22] On March 21, Ito was appointed Minister of the Imperial Household Department and became chairman of the *Seido Torishirabe Kyoku*.[23] He selected nine assistants, the most important of which were Ito

---

19. Kiyomizu, *op. cit.*, 318-319.
20. Much later Ito wrote of his tour in a rather misleading fashion, claiming that he took an "extended journey in different countries to make as thorough a study as possible of the actual workings of different systems of constitutional government, of their various provisions, as well as of theories and opinions actually entertained by influential persons on the actual stage itself of constitutional life." *Fifty Years of New Japan*, I, 127.
21. Until his death, Iwakura had remained concerned about the application of Western political theory to Japanese government, for he felt that a Japanese constitution should not be based solely upon European systems of government. Specifically, he wanted to be sure that the Emperor was properly fitted into a constitutional system of government. When Ito suggested that he might engage a German scholar to aid in drafting a constitution, Iwakura advised that the scholar first be made familiar with Japanese history and customs and, in March 1883, he went so far as to propose that the government compile a history of Japan to be translated into German. The Emperor approved the project, and in April, the government established the *Hensan Kyoku* (Bureau of Compilation) in the Imperial Household Department with Iwakura in charge. Unfortunately, the work was barely under way when Iwakura died. Miyakoshi, *Nihon kensei kiso shiryo*, 378-379.
22. McLaren, *Japanese Government Documents*, 87n.
23. *Ibid.*, 87-88.

THE MAKING OF THE MEIJI CONSTITUTION

Myoji, Inouye Kowashi, and Kaneko Kentaro.[24] Work on drafting the constitution was not begun immediately, however, because Ito first wanted to carry out several administrative reforms to facilitate the shift to constitutional government.

Ito's first move in this direction was the creation of a new nobility. For some time he had been considering the establishment of a system of peerage to provide the basis for the membership of the upper house of parliament, which Ito hoped to make a check upon the popularly elected lower house.[25] On July 6, 1884, a system of peerage was instituted by the promulgation of two imperial ordinances.[26] The new nobility was modeled on the German system and included a total of five hundred members divided among the five ranks of prince, marquis, count, viscount, and baron. These ranks were bestowed upon members of the court nobility, former *daimyo,* and those former samurai who had rendered meritorious service to the state.[27] There can be no doubt that this was an important practical maneuver, for the Satsuma-Choshu oligarchy institutionalized the support of many of the former rulers of Japan. In reality, the new peerage was the culmination of a series of changes that had transformed the former *daimyo* from territorial feudal lords into landlord-capitalist cliques that generally supported the policies of the oligarchy.[28]

---

24. Fujii, *Nihon kempo seitei shi,* 291.
25. These sentiments were expressed by Ito in a letter to Ito Myoji on September 14, 1881. He stated: "I believe that [the creation of a peerage] is an absolutely indispensable instrument for fortifying the position of the Imperial House. . . . We are both worried about the recent tendency of both the government and the people to slip unknowing into the spirit of republicanism. If we do nothing about it, and it finally reaches an irredeemable situation, no matter how good a plan we have, it will be useless. Therefore, I hope to find a way to save the situation by taking advantage of the fact that as yet the afterglow of the feudalistic pro-Emperor sentiment has not yet completely died down [and create a peerage] even though this is contrary to the spirit of the times and goes against the feelings of the people. I hope you will support me in this." *Ito Hirobumi den* (Tokyo, 1940), II, 218, cited in Ike, *Political Democracy,* 172.
26. McLaren, *Japanese Government Documents,* 88-90.
27. For a summary of the distribution of the five ranks, see McLaren, *Japanese Government Documents,* 88n. It is interesting to note that the heirs of Kido and Okubo were made marquis, while Ito, Yamagata, Inouye Kaoru, Oki, Yamada, and Hirosawa became counts. That the government intended to create a body favorable to its policies is evident from the fact that Goto, Itagaki, and Okuma were overlooked. For a complete listing of the new nobility, see *Japan Weekly Mail,* August 2, 1884, 117-122.
28. Hirano Gitaro, *Nihon shihonshugi shakai no kato* (Tokyo, 1934), 259n.

Drafting the Constitution, 1881-1889

The second major reform was the establishment of a modern cabinet. By imperial decree, on December 22, 1885, the offices of *Dajodaijin, Udaijin, Sadaijin,* Councillor, and Minister were supplanted by a Prime Minister and Ministers of State.[29] Sanjo, the retiring *Dajodaijin*,[30] explained that the establishment of a cabinet was a return to ancient Japanese political theory by which the Emperor personally ruled, receiving reports from his ministers and deciding all matters by and with his ministers' advice. Sanjo wrote: "The cabinet should be made a supreme council of Ministers with authority to communicate directly with Your Majesty . . . [and] should serve as the hands and feet, the ears and eyes of Your Majesty."

While this official interpretation justified the change in terms of ancient political theory, there were of course more practical reasons for the creation of a modern cabinet system prior to the promulgation of the constitution. Indeed, the oligarchs felt that it was necessary to centralize their powers further in anticipation of the convocation of parliament in 1890. Adequate evidence exists for such a conclusion. An analysis of the personnel of the new cabinet clearly reveals the determination of the Satsuma-Choshu oligarchs to consolidate their political power. Only two of the ten posts in the cabinet were awarded to "outside" men, while the remaining eight were equally divided between the former samurai of the two *han*.[31] For the first time, a Prime Minister was responsible to the Emperor for the administration of the entire country; moreover, all department ministers were subject to his

---

29. McLaren, *Japanese Government Documents*, 94-95, 98.
30. *Ibid.*, 90-93. After his resignation, Sanjo was appointed Lord Keeper of the Privy Seal, a new office created by the reorganization.
31. Choshu: Ito (Prime Minister), Inouye Kaoru (Foreign Affairs), Yamagata (Home Affairs), Mori (Education); Satsuma: Matsukata (Finance), Oyama (War), Saigo (Navy), Yamada (Justice). The exceptions were Tani Kanjo (Tosa), Minister of Agriculture, and Enomoto Takeaki (Hizen), Minister of Communications. Osatake, *Nihon kensei shi taiko*, II, 714. Essentially, this is the same administration as the cabinet in office at the time of the promulgation of the constitution. The only changes were as follows: Kuroda became Prime Minister, replacing Ito, who was appointed President of the Privy Council; Okuma became Minister of Foreign Affairs, replacing Inouye Kaoru, who became Minister of Agriculture and Finance.

direct supervision and were at the same time accountable to him for all the affairs of their respective departments.[32]

The last major reform enacted by the oligarchy in preparation for constitutional government was the formation of the civil service in December 1885. This initiated a shift in the appointment of officials below the two highest ranks in the bureaucracy[33] from a "spoils system" to a merit system based upon examinations. However, present officeholders were frozen in their positions, and graduates of Tokyo Imperial University were exempted from the civil service examinations.[34] As a result of this exemption, the regulations virtually turned the university into a training school for a highly conservative bureaucracy which in time came to have a vested interest in government.[35]

---

32. To Ito, the cabinet would be the most important political body in the state and the Prime Minister the most powerful single figure. Ito stated: "In our opinion the essence of Government lies in the establishment of a sound system of administration, and in a wide use of opportunities. Similarly, what is essential to a Cabinet is that it should have direct control of all affairs of state. . . ." McLaren, *Japanese Government Documents*, 96-97. In his commentaries, Ito also suggested the reason for the change from the *Dajokan* to the cabinet system modeled upon the Prussian cabinet of Bismarck. He stated: "By the said reorganization, the Ministers of State were made each separately to bear his share of responsibility to the Emperor directly. Over them was placed the Minister President of State. The object of this change was, on the one hand, to give weight to the functions of the Ministers of State and to impress upon them a higher sense of their responsibility and, on the other, to maintain the unity of the Cabinet and to avoid all complications and variances therein. . . . The Minister President of State is to make representations to the Emperor on matters of state and to indicate, according to His pleasure, the general course of the policy of the State, every branch of the administration being under the control of the said Minister. The compass of his duties is large and his responsibility cannot but be proportionally great." *Commentaries on the Constitution of the Empire of Japan*, translated by Ito Myoji (2nd edition, Tokyo, 1906), 99, 103. Ito's view of the position of the Prime Minister was stated officially by the imperial notification of December 24, 1889. McLaren, *Japanese Government Documents*, 232-233.

33. For details, see Harold Quigley, *Japanese Government and Politics* (New York, 1932), 143; and McLaren, *Japanese Government Documents*, 103-108.

34. By 1881, Tokyo University, which had been founded in 1877, had become the most preferred and important institution for training prospective bureaucrats. In 1881, the university was reorganized, and its president was made an appointee of the government, directly responsible to the Minister of Education. The university faculty, under the influence of Prussian education, became civil servants. In March 1886, Tokyo University became Tokyo Imperial University, with the announced primary purpose of teaching and investigating those fields of science and learning which were of practical service to the needs of the state. Tokyo Imperial University, *Tokyo teikoku daigaku gojunenshi* (Tokyo, 1932), I, 505-506, 932, cited in Norman, *Feudal Background of Japanese Politics*, 93.

35. The advantages of the Tokyo Imperial University graduates were bitterly criticized by the political parties that were formed in the early 1890's, and in 1893 this exemption was withdrawn. In 1898, during the short-lived tenure of the party cabinet of Okuma and Itagaki, the civil service system was modified by the application of the party spoils system. However, in 1899, the succeeding government of Yamagata enacted three imperial ordinances which tightened official discipline, regularized the examination system

Drafting the Constitution, 1881-1889

By 1886, Ito and his committee were able to turn to the problem of drafting a constitution which would provide a new legal sanction for the reorganized imperial government as well as limit the powers of parliament. As a guide for the members of the committee to whom he delegated most of the work, Ito outlined the constitutional policy of the oligarchs. He emphasized that, in accordance with the development of Japanese history, the Emperor would remain as the source of political power in the state. Ito conceded that the constitution in form would be based on the constitutions of Prussia and the various German states, but he insisted that the "spirit" behind it would be Japanese. He cautioned them to draft a short document and to work out separately the details of politics and administration in an Imperial House Law, a Law of the Houses, an Election Law for the House of Representatives, and an Ordinance for the House of Peers. Finally, Ito discussed the limits of the power of parliament and the nature of cabinet responsibility.[36]

Ito divided the work of drafting the constitution and the accompanying laws among the members of the *Seido Torishirabe Kyoku,* who would consult with one another on important points. Inouye Kowashi was placed in charge of the constitution and the Imperial House Law. In Ito's mind, Inouye was an excellent choice; a fellow clansman, he was familiar with the constitutional government of Prussia and the German States as a result of his studies with the German jurist Hermann Roessler, who was then teaching law at Tokyo Imperial University.[37] Ito Myoji, also from

---

and terms of tenure, and sealed off the bureaucracy completely from political influence by prohibiting members of political parties from holding government positions below that of cabinet minister. Quigley, *op. cit.,* 143-144.

36. Osatake, *Nihon kensei shi taiko,* II, 717-719; Fujii Shinichi, *Teikoku kempo to Kaneko haku* (Tokyo, 1942), 266-269, 272.

37. In 1875, Inouye had translated the Prussian constitution into Japanese, and in 1881, under Iwakura's order, he drafted a constitution based on that of Prussia in consultation with Roessler. Suzuki, *Nihon kempo shi gaisetsu,* 286-287. For the relationship between Inouye and Roessler, see *Meiji bunka zenshu,* XXII, 217-236. There is another constitution drafted by Inouye, which includes an article-by-article commentary on the constitutional practices of the various nations of Europe. This document, which is undated but is thought to have been written before 1881, is included in Ito, *Kempo shiryo,* II, 1-53. For a discussion of it, see Suzuki, *Nihon kempo shi gaisetsu,* 457.

Choshu, was assigned to work out a law for the organization of parliament. The last member, Kaneko Kentaro, was delegated to frame an election law for the House of Representatives and to plan the organization of the House of Peers.[38] While Ito and Inouye were longtime friends of Ito, Kaneko had come to Ito's attention as a result of his treatise on constitutional government that the *Genroin* had sent to Ito while he was in Europe.[39]

In preparing the draft constitution, Inouye sought the advice of his friend and teacher Roessler, and to a lesser extent of Albert Mosse, who had come to Japan at Ito's request as an adviser on local government. To keep Ito informed of their progress, Inouye worked out an interesting technique. He wrote questions in English which Roessler and Mosse answered in English, and for Ito's instruction these questions and answers were then translated into Japanese.[40] From the outset, Inouye and Roessler adhered to the principle of making the Emperor the source of political power. In addition, Roessler emphasized the need for investing him with specific executive and legislative powers.[41] Opposed to representative government, Roessler also advocated that the Ministers of State should be responsible to the Emperor and not to parliament.[42] Ito and Inouye, of course, agreed with these views wholeheartedly; they rejected, however, his advice that the Emperor actually direct the cabinet on the pretext that this was already

---

38. Osatake, *Nihon kensei shi taiko*, II, 724.

39. From 1871-1878, Kaneko studied law in the United States at Harvard Law School. In 1881, he published *Seijiron ryaku* (Political thought in brief), a survey of the development of Japanese political thought. After Ito's departure for Europe, Kaneko became a member of a *Genroin* committee which was assigned to investigate the various principles of constitutional government that had been given to Ito as a guide. The result of Kaneko's work was a written report on constitutional government, *Kakkoku kempo ido kamoku* (Items of difference in the constitutions of various nations), which was a functional description of constitutional government. This work was forwarded to Ito, who was deeply impressed by Kaneko's knowledge and ability. Fujii, *Teikoku kempo to Kaneko haku*, 228-233; Fujii, *Nihon kempo seitei shi*, 289-290; Osatake, *Nihon kensei shi taiko*, II, 667.

40. For an example of these "conversations" between Inouye, Roessler, and Mosse, see Ito, *Kempo shiryo*, I, 306-511, and *ibid.*, III, 178-195.

41. *Ibid.*, I, 118-171. For an excellent summary of Roessler's view of the role of the Emperor in government, see either Suzuki, *Nihon kempo shi gaisetsu*, 152-157; Osatake, *Nihon kensei shi taiko*, II, 132-136; or Fujii, *Teikoku kempo to Kaneko haku*, 295-313. Regarding the ordinance power of the Emperor, see Ito, *Kempo shiryo*, I, 423-424.

42. Ito, *Kempo shiryo*, I, 385-388.

implied in the imperial system.[43] Finally, Roessler rendered valuable assistance on matters of government finance. He urged Ito and Inouye to follow Prussian and German precedents and not depend absolutely upon parliamentary approval of the budget. He recommended that the cabinet be allowed to fall back on the budget of the previous year in case of a failure to gain the consent of parliament.[44] Roessler cautioned that parliament should not be empowered to alter expenditures or revenues already fixed by laws nor should parliament have any control over imperial expenses.[45] Most of these ideas were already familiar to Ito and Inouye; Roessler's contribution was the conversion of these ideas to particular clauses of the constitution. He was constantly consulted on problems of terminology and meaning.

The work of compiling the constitution entered its second stage on April 30 when Roessler submitted a draft written in German, which was translated into Japanese at Ito's request.[46] In May, Inouye finished two additional drafts: the first of these was based upon the discussions with Roessler and Mosse[47] and the second included a commentary with article-by-article references to the constitutions of Austria (1867), Prussia (1850), Italy (1848), Spain (1845), Belgium, and Portugal.[48] The committee decided that these drafts should provide the basis for further discussion.

In June, the small group moved to Ito's new summer home on the island of Natsushima, near Yokosuka. Ito felt that this secluded spot would provide greater secrecy, and he was determined to avoid adverse criticism or interference resulting from premature publicity regarding the constitution. Because Ito's home was

---

43. *Ibid.*, 358-359, 365.
44. Inouye, under Roessler's influence, had made this point clear to Iwakura earlier and, in 1881, it had been approved by the *Dajokan* as it appeared in the principles submitted by Iwakura. *Supra*, ch. V, note 25.
45. Ito, *Kempo shiryo*, I, 482-484.
46. The Japanese text of Roessler's draft is included in *Meiji bunka zenshu*, IV, 490-496. It is interesting to note that Roessler's statement of the powers of the Emperor is almost identical with that which appears in the Meiji Constitution.
47. For this draft, see Ito, *Kempo shiryo*, I, 649-672. For the convenience of Ito and the rest, Inouye also summarized his discussions with Roessler and Mosse in a commentary in each article of the draft. *Ibid.*, 306-511.
48. This draft and commentary are included in *ibid.*, 511-649.

very small, Ito Myoji, Inouye, and Kaneko resided in a nearby town; but when a briefcase containing Roessler's draft was stolen in early August, the three men moved into Ito's home as a security measure.[49] Throughout the summer of 1887, the small group deliberated over the draft constitutions of Roessler and Inouye, and in September a fourth draft was finished.[50] After a careful examination of this draft by Roessler, who made several suggestions regarding terminology, the group undertook a final revision; however, this task was interrupted when Ito departed for a tour of Kyushu and Okinawa, and deliberations were not resumed until early in 1888.[51] Finally, in April, drafts of the constitution and of the Imperial House Law were completed and ready for ratification.[52]

The procedure to be used in ratification had been an important political issue ever since the 1881 announcement of the government's intention to establish a parliament, and the leaders of the moribund political parties had continued to agitate for a constitutional convention. This argument was rejected by a majority of the oligarchs, who felt that approval by the Emperor would be adequate.[53] However, in the summer and fall of 1887, there was a temporary revival of the democratic movement which was embarrassing to the government. Leaders like Itagaki and Goto attempted to utilize economic discontent and the government's unsuccessful attempts to revise the "unequal treaties" to put pressure on the oligarchs. They organized great political rallies in Tokyo

---

49. *Ito Hirobumi den*, II, 578. Ito was criticized for this move by liberals and conservatives alike. The liberals *(Jiyuronsha)*, fearing an authoritarian regime, called him a Bismarck, while the conservatives claimed that he desired secrecy to draft a constitution based on the example of Great Britain. Suzuki, *Nihon kempo shi gaisetsu*, 446; Osatake, *Nihon kensei shi taiko*, 11, 726.

50. The text of this document is included in *Ito Myoji monjo* (Papers of Ito Myoji), to which the author did not have access.

51. It is unfortunate that no record of the discussions is available, but several documents indicate that problems of terminology were constantly arising. Ike cites one example in his *Political Democracy*, 178.

52. The text of the final draft is included in Suzuki, *Nihon kempo shi gaisetsu*, 491-497. A commentary on it is included in Ito, *Kempo shiryo*, II, 53-207. For an analysis of the Meiji Constitution based upon a comparison of the text with that of the constitutions of Prussia and the various German states, see Nakano Tomio, *The Ordinance Power of the Japanese Emperor* (Baltimore, 1923), 236-252.

53. McLaren, *Japanese Government Documents*, 325-330.

Drafting the Constitution, 1881-1889

and submitted petitions to the government demanding freedom of speech and assembly, reduction of the land-tax, and revision of the treaties. In October 1887, Goto organized the short-lived *Daido Danketsu* (Union at Large) in an attempt to merge the defunct political parties for the common purpose of opposing the oligarchs in parliament.[54]

When this anti-government agitation increased throughout the fall of 1887, Yamagata, the Minister of Home Affairs, acted resolutely. Under his orders, the police enforced regulations restricting the right to present petitions and to hold public meetings and, on December 14, the Home Ministry issued a new set of regulations prohibiting the attendance of government employees at political gatherings.[55] When these measures proved inadequate, the drastic Peace Preservation Law was drafted and promulgated on December 25.[56] By its terms, secret societies and political meetings were forbidden, and the police were given authority to close meetings at their own discretion. More important, however, was the provision which empowered the police to banish the political enemies of the oligarchs from Tokyo.[57] Over five hundred persons deemed dangerous to the public peace were ordered to leave Tokyo immediately.[58]

It was against this background of political agitation and repression that Ito had to decide upon a method of ratification for the draft constitution and the accompanying laws. It is understandable that he rejected the democratic demand for ratification by a constitutional convention of delegates elected by the people, but at the same time he rejected the conservative suggestion that approval by the Emperor would be sufficient. It is clear also that

---

54. Goto continued as head of the union until February 1889, when he joined the government as Minister of Communications, leaving his followers in the lurch. For an excellent summary of the revival of the democratic movement, see Ike, *Political Democracy*, 181-187.
55. McLaren, *Japanese Government Documents*, 504.
56. For the circumstances attending the implementation of this law, see Ike, *Political Democracy*, 185.
57. McLaren, *Japanese Government Documents*, 502-504.
58. For a partial listing of the more important political personages ordered out of Tokyo, see Okuma, *Fifty Years of New Japan*, 160. For other oppressive legislation, see McLaren, *Japanese Government Documents*, 543-550, 551-557.

he considered ratification by the *Genroin* as a possible solution, but he was apprehensive that the *Genroin* would seek to alter the draft constitution. Fnally, he decided that the constitution should be ratified by a special organization, and he selected for this purpose the Privy Council, which had been established by imperial ordinance on April 28, 1888, the very month that the final draft of the constitution had been completed.[59] On April 30, just two days later, Ito became President of the Privy Council, resigning the post of Prime Minister, which was bestowed upon Kuroda; moreover, Ito's three assistants were appointed secretaries of the Privy Council. Membership in the Council was by imperial appointment and, in practice, it was confined to male members of the imperial family, peers, and cabinet ministers.[60]

The deliberations of the Privy Council began in May 1888 and continued until January 1889. During this time, the Council met in forty-one regular sessions and three special meetings, all but one of which were held in the presence of the Emperor. These discussions were conducted in secret, and every effort was made to prevent information from leaking out.[61] Commencing with the Imperial House Law, the constitution, the Law of the Houses of the Diet, the Law of Election, the Imperial Ordinance concerning the House of Peers were all discussed and approved in order.[62]

The act of promulgation alone remained, and again the government made excellent use of the Emperor. February 11, 1889, was chosen as the day for the promulgation ceremony, for this was the anniversary of the accession of the Emperor Jimmu. High government officials, foreign diplomats, and a few prominent

---

59. McLaren, *Japanese Government Documents*, 127-132.
60. For a list of the personnel of the Privy Council that ratified the constitution, see Osatake, *Nihon kensei shi taiko*, II, 768-769.
61. *Ibid.*, 769. Evidently, secrecy was suggested by Kaneko, who had discovered that the American constitution had been discussed in secret.
62. The secrecy of the Privy Council deliberations has made it difficult to determine what influence the Privy Council had in amending the draft submitted by Ito. While very few documents are available, a comparison of the draft and the final text reveals only a few significant changes. Both houses of parliament were permitted to initiate legislation, and both houses were given equal power with regard to finance.

DRAFTING THE CONSTITUTION, 1881-1889

citizens assembled at the imperial palace in the presence of the Emperor, who read a prepared statement granting a constitution to the people of the nation.[63] In this brief ceremony, which probably lasted no more than ten minutes, all the work of Ito and his associates was realized. That the Emperor's declaration was read to the oligarchs and not to the public was perhaps a fitting climax to the highly secretive methods by which the constitution had been drafted and ratified.[64]

---

63. McLaren, *Japanese Government Documents*, 113-114.
64. The public did participate in a limited fashion, for the occasion was made one of national celebration; however, the government was careful to prevent public criticism of the ceremony and the constitution. The publication of several Tokyo newspapers was suspended, and others were warned not to criticize the constitution. Ike, *Political Democracy*, 188.

Chapter VII
The Oligarchy and the Meiji Constitution

While the oligarchs made important political concessions to those groups that demanded a national parliament, the Meiji Constitution[1] was essentially a carefully formulated legal justification for a government in which the oligarchs had only a minimum of responsibility to the people. By the Meiji Constitution, the oligarchs established a body of authoritarian political principles in Western forms as the ultimate defense of their dominant position in the government. The basic premise of these principles was the doctrine that supreme political power rested in the person of the Emperor; moreover, the Meiji Constitution emphasized that the Emperor was the center of political power not by divine right but by divine descent. The preamble to the constitution stated: "The rights of sovereignty of the State, We have inherited from Our Ancestors, and We shall bequeath them to our descendants," and Article 4 of the constitution added: "The Emperor is the head of the Empire, combining in Himself the rights of sovereignty, and exercises them, according to the provisions of the present constitution."[2]

---

1. The text of the Meiji Constitution, as it appears in McLaren, *Japanese Government Documents,* 136-144, is included in Appendix X. For the laws that were promulgated at the same time as the constitution, the "Law of the Houses," the "Imperial Ordinance concerning the House of Peers," "The Imperial House Law," and "The Law of Elections," see *ibid.,* 156-170, 153-156, 145-153, 171-211.

2. With regard to this doctrine, Ito stated: "The Sacred Throne of Japan is inherited from the Imperial Ancestors, and is to be bequeathed to posterity; in it resides the power to reign over and govern the state." In commenting on the fact that the constitution did define the channels through which the imperial power was exercised and that thereby the Emperor's power was not arbitrary, Ito added: "That express opinions concerning the sovereign power are especially mentioned in the Articles of the Constitution, in no wise implies that any newly settled opinion therein is set forth by the Constitution; on the contrary, the original national polity is by no means changed by it, but is more strongly confirmed than ever." *Commentaries,* 2. This question of sovereignty subsequently became a center of controversy. Professor Minobe of the Law Faculty of Tokyo Imperial University denied that sovereignty rested in the person of the Emperor; instead, he viewed the Emperor as an organ of the state under the constitution. On the other hand, the doctrine of "imperial sovereignty" was defended by his colleague, Professor Uesugi, who equated the Emperor with the state. Professor Uesugi further argued that since the

The Oligarchy and the Constitution

The oligarchs also made certain that this doctrine was beyond the possibility of constitutional change by including a clause in the Imperial House Law which provided for uninterrupted imperial succession to the sovereignty of the state.[3] With regard to amending the constitution, Article 73 provided that the Emperor alone had the power to initiate action. The preamble to the constitution stated: "When in the future it may be necessary to amend any of the provisions of the present Constitution, We or Our successors shall assume the initiative right, and submit a project for the same to the Imperial Diet. The Imperial Diet shall pass its vote upon it, according to the conditions imposed by the present Constitution, and in no way otherwise shall Our descendants or Our subjects be permitted to attempt any alteration thereof."

The oligarchs also attempted to gain popular acceptance of their contention regarding imperial sovereignty by religious and ethical arguments. During the early years of the Meiji period, they had re-established Shinto as the state religion in order to emphasize the supreme position of the Emperor in government and to popularize the idea that this position was based upon a divine inheritance.[4] Indeed, the Meiji Constitution was the culmination of that emphasis in Japanese society on loyalty that had begun in the feudal period and had been successfully transformed into a patriotism based upon loyalty to the Emperor. Furthermore, in the imperial rescript on education of 1890, the oligarchs exhorted the people to "be filial to your parents, affectionate to your brothers

---

Emperor established the constitution in his own right and held the rights of sovereignty, there could not be an act of the Emperor which was contrary to the constitution. For a discussion of these points of view, see K. Colegrove, "The Japanese Emperor," *American Political Science Review*, XXVI (1932), 642-659, 828-845. For other views on the question, see Quigley, *Japanese Government and Politics*, 67-68.

3. McLaren, *Japanese Government Documents*, 146. Nakano, taking note of the fact that the Imperial House Law was regarded as superior to ordinary legislation and could not be supplanted or amended by such, commented that this was "counter to monarchical constitutional states in which succession to the throne and to regency is regulated either by the constitution or by statutes in order to safeguard the state against the danger of arbitrary changes in the law by the ruler in his dynastic interests." *The Ordinance Power of the Japanese Emperor*, 29.

4. For a discussion of the oligarchs' use of Shinto to bolster the position of the Emperor in the eyes of the people, see D. C. Holtom, *The National Faith of Japan* (London, 1938), 54-70.

and sisters; as husbands and wives be harmonious; as friends true; bear yourselves in modesty and moderation . . . always respect the Constitution and observe the laws; should emergency arise, offer yourselves courageously to the State; and thus guard and maintain the prosperity of Our Imperial Throne coeval with heaven and earth."[5] This interpretation of Confucian philosophy was an attempt to put new vigor into the concept of the Emperor as the father of the nation and the subjects as his children in order to equate political obligations with filial piety. There would thus be no conflict between family and state since loyalty to the state and filial piety were one and the same.[6] At the same time that the government began to function under the Meiji Constitution, the oligarchs invoked the people to respect the Emperor and the constitution and to observe the laws on the basis of morality and the heritage bequeathed by the ancestors of the Emperor.

While the constitution and the ancillary documents stated that the Emperor was the unique source of political power, the oligarchs were careful to have the constitution actually enumerate the specific powers of the Emperor. Articles 11 to 16 conferred on him such broad executive powers as supreme command of the army and navy; the power to declare war, make peace, and conclude treaties; the right to confer titles of nobility, ranks, and orders; and the right to order an amnesty, pardon, and commutation of punishment; moreover, the Emperor was also given important general administrative powers by Article 10, which provided that "the Emperor determines the organization of the different branches of the administration, and salaries of all civil and military officers, and appoints and dismisses the same."

The oligarchs were also careful to establish the legislative superiority of the Emperor over the newly created Diet composed of the House of Peers and the House of Representatives. Article

---

5. Quoted in R. K. Hall, *Shushin: The Ethics of a Defeated Nation* (New York, 1949), 161.
6. As Ike points out, the government had been taking legal and educational steps ever since the Meiji Restoration to impose a family structure on society that was compatible with the state. *Political Democracy*, 197-198.

The Oligarchy and the Constitution

5 of the constitution stated: "The Emperor exercises the legislative power with the consent of the Imperial Diet," but Articles 37 and 38 added: "Every law requires the consent of the Imperial Diet . . . [which] . . . shall vote upon projects of law submitted to it by the government, and may respectively initiate projects of law." However, the Emperor's legislative superiority was established by Article 6, which in practice gave the Emperor an effective veto power over laws passed by the Diet. Article 6 stated: "The Emperor gives sanctions to laws and orders them to be promulgated and executed."[7] If a veto would be inappropriate, the government had the power to delay publishing the act in the *Official Gazette,* which publicly brought the act into effect, or it could fail to provide in the budget the necessary funds to enforce the act.[8] The government also had the power to amend or withdraw any bill that it had introduced for the decision of the Diet.

There were other ways in which the Emperor and the government could influence the legislative process. The Emperor had the power to convoke, open, adjourn, and prorogue the Diet; to dissolve the House of Representatives; to prolong the session of the Diet; to convoke extraordinary sessions of the Diet and determine their length; and to order the Diet to hold secret meetings. Ministers or their delegates had the right to sit and speak in either house and in committee hearings; moreover, the government could bring in bills and declare precedence for them.[9]

The constitution also granted the Emperor ordinance power of an extensive nature. First, he had the power to issue ordinances in cases of national emergencies and financial emergencies.[10] More

---

7. Ito stressed that final legislative authority rested in the person of the Emperor, whom he called "the source and fountainhead of legislative power." *Commentaries,* 9.
8. Robert K. Reischauer, *Japan: Government-Politics* (New York, 1939), 79.
9. McLaren, *Japanese Government Documents,* 136, 160-162.
10. Article 8 stated: "The Emperor, in consequence of an urgent necessity to maintain public safety or to avert public calamities, issues, when the Imperial Diet is not sitting, Imperial Ordinances in the place of law. Such Imperial Ordinances are to be laid before the Imperial Diet at its next session, and when the Diet does not approve the said Ordinances, the Government shall declare them to be invalid for the future." Article 70 stated: "When the Imperial Diet cannot be convoked, owing to the external or internal condition of the country, in case of urgent need for the maintenance of public safety, the Government may take all necessary financial measures, by means of an Imperial Ordinance. In the case mentioned in the preceding clause, the matter shall be submitted to the Imperial Diet at its next session, and its approbation shall be obtained thereto."

important from an ordinary legislative standpoint, however, was the Emperor's power, conferred by Article 9, to issue administrative ordinances "necessary for the carrying out of the laws, or for the maintenance of the public peace and order, and for the promotion of the welfare of the subjects." The only restriction upon this power was the provision that "no ordinance shall in any way alter any of the existing laws."[11] Lastly, the Emperor's broad executive powers enabled him to issue ordinances of a general legislative nature.

The oligarchs made the paramount political power of the Emperor effective by providing for the absolute financial independence of the government as well as the Emperor. Ito feared that parliamentary control of finance would ultimately make the government responsible to the will of the Diet. He also wished to be certain that the Diet would be unable to suspend or repeal existing laws simply by a refusal to vote the funds required for their execution. While Article 64 of the constitution provided that "the expenditure and revenue of the State require the consent of the Imperial Diet by means of an annual budget," the oligarchs utilized the Prussian concept of specifying that expenditures required for the execution of laws were not subject to the actions of the legislature. In this regard, Article 67 stated: "Those already-fixed expenditures[12] based by the Constitution upon the powers

---

11. Ito points out: "Emergency ordinances . . . may take the place of law, but the administrative ordinance . . . shall take effect within the limits of law, and although they can supply the deficiencies of law, yet they shall have no power to either alter any law or to regulate those matters for which a law is required by express provision of the constitution." *Commentaries*, 20-21. However, as Quigley has observed, "In Japan, as in other states, the police power is employed not only to compel obedience to law and to protect the community from disease, fire, and other calamities, but to further the intellectual and material welfare of the people. Thus, if statutory provision is lacking, ordinances may be issued to create and maintain public works; to provide subsidies to individuals and corporations both for the improvement of social conditions and the development of commerce, industry, and other economic interests; to confer upon private enterprise a public character; or to establish charges in kind or money for maintaining public welfare activities." *Japanese Government and Politics*, 121.

12. These expenditures included ordinary administrative expenses, salaries of officials, expenses arising from treaties, interest on the national debt, subsidies, pensions, etc. See "The Interpretation of the Sixty-Seventh Article of the Constitution" in McLaren, *Japanese Government Documents*, 233-236. With regard to new expenditures, Ito wrote: "From the wording 'Already-fixed expenditures,' it is to be understood, that in regard to new expenditures or to the increase of existing ones, though based on the sovereign powers of the Emperor, the Diet may have the power to freely deliberate upon them." *Commentaries*, 142-143.

appertaining to the Emperor, and such expenditures as may have arisen by the effect of law, or that appertain to the legal obligations of the government, shall be neither rejected nor reduced by the Imperial Diet, without the concurrence of the government." Finally, in case the Diet failed to pass the budget, Article 71 empowered the government to carry out the budget of the previous year. With regard to taxes, Article 63 continued those levied prior to the promulgation of the constitution; however, Article 62 provided that "the imposition of a new tax or the modification of the rates [of an existing one] shall be determined by law." Thus the government was not dependent upon the Diet for an annual vote of revenues; however, new taxation could not be levied without the Diet's consent.

The Imperial House Law provided for the financial independence of the Emperor. Article 45 stipulated that "no landed property or other property, that has been fixed as Imperial Hereditary Estates, shall be divided up and alienated."[13] Article 66 added: "The expenditures of the Imperial House shall be defrayed every year out of the National Treasury, according to the present fixed amount for the same, and shall not require the consent thereto of the Imperial Diet, except in case an increase thereof is found necessary."[14]

While the Meiji Constitution invested supreme political power in the person of the Emperor, he did not actually take part in the administration of the government. Instead, he ruled through his Ministers of State.[15] Since the Diet was weak, this meant, for

---

13. McLaren, *Japanese Government Documents*, 151.

14. In 1881, the imperial lands consisted of only 634 *cho* (one *cho* is equal to 2.45 acres), but by 1890 they comprised over 3,500,000 *cho*. In 1882, the imperial family held private funds totaling 1,700,000 yen, and by 1887, with the addition of valuable securities, these revenues amounted to over 7,500,000 yen. Besides the income from this land and investments, the imperial family was granted an annual appropriation of 3,000,000 yen. Yamada Seitaro, *Nihon shihonshugi bunseki* (Tokyo, 1935), 185.

15. Asakawa, commenting on this, states: "The cabinet is the organ, through which the Emperor's sovereignty is manifested. In the practical operation of government, the Emperor is not expected to manifest a will of his own, except in so far as he may persuade his ministers to alter what they had decided. The oligarchs were able to point to the historical precedent of an unwritten law more than a thousand years old that ... politically, he [the Emperor] shall be impersonal and let properly constituted authorities act as his responsible ministers." Asakawa Kanichi, "Some Contributions of Feudal Japan to the New Japan," *Journal of Race Development*, III (1912), 30.

all practical purposes, that the influential leaders of Choshu and Satsuma controlled the government through their positions in the cabinet, the supreme command, the Privy Council, and the Imperial Household Ministry, all of which constituted the actual repositories of executive power. Thus the Meiji Constitution, from one point of view, established an oligarchical clan control in a modern political form.

Once the Meiji Constitution was put into operation, the oligarchy tended to become institutionalized as a special executive body, known later as the *genro*.[16] Individually, the oligarchs held important offices of state, civil and military, and, as a group, they tended to form an extra-constitutional advisory council which in reality governed the country. Such a body was absolutely necessary to enable the government to function smoothly, for with several executive agencies "advising" the Emperor independently, the *genro* constituted the only political authority able to make final decisions; moreover, in the operation of government, the *genro* provided a basic continuity among these several agencies by virtue of the dominant position of its members in each.[17]

The cabinet, which was the most important of the executive agencies, was not specifically mentioned in the constitution. Article 55 merely provided: "The respective Ministers of State shall give their advice to the Emperor and be responsible for it." However, the cabinet was recognized by Article 76 which reiterated the legality of those enactments which had established and enumerated the functions and powers of the cabinet. Most important of those enactments was the imperial notification of December 1889, which enumerated seven categories of matters which were required to be submitted to the cabinet.

---

16. Iwasaki states that the term *genro* was first applied in 1900. *Working Forces in Japanese Politics* (New York, 1921), 38. This was the inevitable result of the fact that once the constitution defined the organs of government, the public began to realize that an extra-constitutional body of statesmen settled the affairs of the nation.

17. Until 1918, with only one exception, the *genro* controlled the cabinet through their monopoly over the office of Prime Minister. See Reischauer, *Japan: Government-Politics*, 107. The *genro* also controlled the Privy Council through their near-monopoly over the office of president and their role in approving the appointment of members. In the military-naval sphere, the four most powerful men were *genro*: Yamagata, Oyama, Katsura, and Matsukata.

The Oligarchy and the Constitution

1. Drafts of laws,[18] financial estimates, and settled accounts.
2. Treaties with foreign countries and all national questions of importance.
3. Ordinances relating to administration, or to the carrying out of regulations and laws.
4. Disputes connected with the relative competence of Ministers of Departments.
5. Petitions from the people, handed down from the Throne or submitted by the Imperial Diet.
6. Expenditures apart from ordinary estimates (budget).
7. Appointments of *chokunin* officials and of Prefects and Governors, as well as their promotions and removals.[19]

The cabinet's power stemmed from the fact that it was not responsible to the Diet. While the constitution was not absolutely clear regarding ministerial responsibility,[20] in the practical operation of government the cabinet recognized only responsibility to the Emperor. Ito, in defense of ministerial responsibility to the Emperor, stated: "He [the sovereign] alone can dismiss a minister who has been appointed by him. Who then is it, except the Sovereign, that can appoint, dismiss, and punish a Minister of State? The appointment and dismissal of them having been included by the Constitution in the sovereign power of the Emperor, it is only a legitimate consequence that the power of deciding as to the responsibility of ministers is withheld from the Diet." Ito did concede that "although the Emperor reserves to Himself in the Constitution the right of appointing his Ministers at His pleasure, in making an appointment the susceptibilities of the public mind must also be taken into consideration. This may be regarded as an indirect method of controlling the responsibility of Ministers." Evidently, Ito had in mind a dual responsibility,

---

18. In 1890, the cabinet established a Legislative Bureau to draft laws and ordinances in accordance with the orders of the Prime Minister and to examine, give opinions on, and amend drafts of laws or ordinances submitted for the discussion of the cabinet by Ministers of State. McLaren, *Japanese Government Documents*, 247-249.

19. *Ibid.*, 232-233. This notification also provided that "in addition to the above, any important matters connected with the duties of Ministers of Departments, and having relation to the higher branches of the Administration, shall also be submitted for deliberation by the Cabinet." The cabinet was also consulted upon matters regulated by the Imperial House Law such as the succession to the throne or the setting up of a regency.

20. Article 55 simply stated: "The respective Ministers of State shall give their advice to the Emperor, and be responsible for it."

primary to the Emperor, and secondary to the people, for he stated: "Ministers are directly responsible to the Emperor, and indirectly so to the people, [but] . . . it is the Sovereign and not the people that can decide as to the responsibility of Ministers, because the Sovereign possesses the rights of sovereignty of the state."[21] Finally, Ito denied the idea of the absolute joint responsibility of the cabinet, for he feared the development of party control over a unified cabinet;[22] however, in reality, the cabinet was closely unified, with results equivalent to those obtained by recognition of joint responsibility.

The supreme command, consisting of the Ministers of War and Navy as well as the two chiefs of staff, was another executive agency independent of legislative or popular control; moreover, it was beyond the control of the cabinet. Paragraph seven of the 1889 imperial notification regarding the cabinet stated: "With the exception of military or naval affairs of grave importance which, having been reported directly to the Sovereign by the Chief of Staff, may have been submitted by His Majesty for the consideration of the Cabinet, the Ministers of State for War and Navy shall report to the [Prime Minister]."[23] Thus, as Quigley points out, "The Ministers of War and the Navy have a dual status. They are members of the cabinet, reporting on general affairs, including some of a military character, through the [Prime Minister]. They

---

21. Ito, *Commentaries*, 102-103. One could go further and point out that in the early years of government under the Meiji Constitution, responsibility to the Emperor meant essentially responsibility to such leading "clan" statesmen as Ito, Yamagata, and Katsura. Quigley, *Japanese Government and Politics*, 90.

22. Ito, *Commentaries*, 103-105. As Quigley points out, "Ito contemplated individual responsibility of cabinet ministers for matters pertaining to their respective departments, joint responsibility for general matters, and responsibility of the [Prime Minister] for both types of decisions." *Japanese Government and Politics*, 83.

23. McLaren, *Japanese Government Documents*, 233. The division between civilian and military in the government had been fostered by General Yamagata, who served as Chief of Staff at different periods and dominated the post since it was invariably filled by one of his subordinates. As early as 1878, Yamagata sponsored the creation of a General Staff Office, which was separate from the cabinet. The Chief of Staff was given direct access to the Emperor and sole responsibility for carrying out military commands. An imperial ordinance issued in January 1882 made it unequivocally clear that the power of the supreme military command was vested in the Emperor; moreover, by 1885, the government recognized the Chief of Staff's right of direct appeal to the throne. Matsushita Yoshio, *Meiji gunsei shi ronshu* (Collected essays in the history of the Meiji military system) (Tokyo, 1938), 78-82, cited in Norman, *Feudal Background of Japanese Politics*, 82.

are also members of the supreme command, reporting directly and independently of their colleagues in the cabinet." An imperial ordinance issued in 1894 further provided that these two posts had to be filled by high military and naval officers respectively.[24] This latter provision ultimately kept the army and navy under the direct control of the Satsuma-Choshu oligarchs and gave them an additional control over the cabinet, since to maintain a cabinet without these two posts was impossible.[25]

The Privy Council was sanctioned by the Meiji Constitution in much the same manner as was the cabinet. Article 56 stated: "The Privy Councillors shall, in accordance with the provisions for the organization of the Privy Council, deliberate upon important matters of State, when they have been consulted by the Emperor." Article 76 continued in force those enactments which pertained to the Privy Council. The imperial ordinance of 1888 which had established the Privy Council was amended in 1890 in order to make the functions and powers of the Privy Council more definite and restricted. However, the Privy Council still exercised influence over the fields of legislation and treatymaking as well as the policies concerned with the organization and powers of the executive.[26] Thus the Privy Council remained as the highest body of the Emperor's constitutional advisers, and, according to Ito, it was "entrusted with the task of planning farsighted schemes of statecraft and of effecting new enactments, after a careful deliberation and calm reflection, by instituting thorough investigation into ancient and modern history, and by consulting scientific principles. . . ."[27] The oligarchs maintained their control of this

---

24. Quigley, *Japanese Government and Politics*, 89.
25. The justification for the measures that established the independent position of the military was based upon Article 11 of the constitution which stated: "The Emperor determines the organization and peace standing of the army and navy."
26. For Article 6 of the ordinance of 1890 which outlined the functions of the Privy Council, see Quigley, *Japanese Government and Politics*, 91-92. The Imperial House Law also gave the Privy Council the power to advise the Emperor on such matters as the order of succession, the establishment of a regency, and the amendment of the Imperial House Law. For a discussion of the organization and powers of the Privy Council, see K. Colegrove, "The Japanese Privy Council," *American Political Science Review*, XXV (1931), 589-614, 881-905.
27. Ito, *Commentaries*, 108-109.

The Making of the Meiji Constitution

body in a number of ways. Most important was their near-monopoly over the powerful post of president;[28] moreover, members were appointed by the Prime Minister in consultation with the *genro*. Finally, cabinet ministers were automatically appointed as Councillors.

The oligarchs also kept a close control over the Imperial Household Ministry. Such posts as the Lord Keeper of the Privy Seal and the Grand Chamberlain were especially important in the eyes of the oligarchs, since these officials were the personal confidants of the Emperor. It was through these men, who were not part of the cabinet or subject to cabinet control, that governmental projects and decisions were reported to the Emperor. From the outset, the Imperial Household Ministry was dominated by "clan" bureaucrats who were usually Privy Councillors or members of the House of Peers.[29]

Another repository of authoritarianism in the government under the Meiji Constitution was in the provisions that defined the rights of Japanese subjects. A "bill of rights," which resembled that of many Western constitutions, was embodied in Chapter II of the constitution; however, these rights were subject to limitations imposed by law. Thus laws restricting freedom of the press and freedom of association were not directly prohibited by the constitution; moreover, the absence of any process such as *habeas corpus* limited individual freedoms. The rights of Japanese subjects were also curtailed by the lack of legislative control over the police ordinance power. Finally, as Quigley points out, "There [was] a distinction . . . between administrative and ordinary matters according to which an official [was] not amenable to the ordinary courts for acts within his competence."[30]

---

28. Ito, Saionji, Kuroda, Oki, and Yamagata held the post. The latter was President from 1905 to 1922.

29. *Japan Chronicle* (Kobe), March 3, 1921, 298, cited in Quigley, *Japanese Government and Politics*, 99.

30. Article 61 of the constitution stated: "No suit which relates to rights alleged to have been infringed by the illegal measures of the executive authorities, and which should come within the competency of the Court of Administrative Litigation, specially established by law, shall be taken cognizance of by a court of law." Uyehara, recognizing the implication of this provision, states: "There is nothing in the constitution to safeguard

The Oligarchy and the Constitution

The Meiji Constitution was the oligarchs' ultimate solution to the general problem of government that faced Japan after the collapse of the Tokugawa feudal system. In this broad context, the Meiji Constitution was a political highpoint in the destruction of feudalism and the rise of capitalism as well as in the emergence of a fervent nationalism during the nineteenth century. In a narrower political sense, the Meiji Constitution was basically a compromise embodying a feudal-based authoritarian political philosophy and the democratic movement's demand for representative government. While the oligarchs did establish a parliament, they were able to place adequate checks upon the powers of the legislature. Applying the doctrine that sovereignty rested in the person of a divine Emperor, they established a government in which they consolidated their control as the Emperor's ministers. Thus, in the final analysis, through their dominant position in the cabinet, the supreme command, the Privy Council, and the Imperial Household Ministry, the oligarchs sought to maintain their power in modern political forms sanctioned by a written constitution and buttressed by a renewed emphasis upon Shinto and orthodox Confucianism.

---

the rights and liberties of the people from the encroachment of the permanent executive officials." George E. Uyehara, *The Political Development of Japan 1867-1909* (London, 1910), 132. Writing much later on the same problem, Nakano states: "Although, with the ever-increasing mass of legislation in recent years, the police ordinances issued under Article 9 have been to a great extent superseded by statutes, liberty still remains as insecure as before. This insecurity of liberty is due to three facts: lack of elaborate statutory control of the police power, lack of judicial remedy against illegal acts of the police authorities, and lack of the participation of local self-government in the administration of police matters." *The Ordinance Power of the Japanese Emperor,* 14.

Bibliography

A. PRIMARY SOURCES

Ito Hirobumi, ed. *Commentaries on the Constitution of the Empire of Japan.* Second edition, Tokyo, 1906. Translated from the Japanese by Ito Myoji.

———. *Kempo Shiryo* (Materials on the Constitution). 3 vols. Tokyo, 1934.

"Kogisho nisshi gianroku" (Proceedings of the discussion and bills of the *Kogisho*). *Meiji bunka zenshu,* IV, 5-161.

McLaren, W. W., ed. "Japanese Government Documents." *Transactions of the Asiatic Society of Japan,* First Series, XLII (1914).

Miyakoshi Shinichiro, ed. *Nihon kensei kiso shiryo* (Basic historical materials on Japanese constitutional government). Tokyo, 1939.

Robinson, James H. "Constitution of the Kingdom of Prussia." *Annals of the American Academy of Political and Social Science,* V (1884), 197-250.

"Rosurerushi togi" (Replies of Roessler). *Meiji bunka zenshu,* XXII, 217-236.

"Seitetsu yumemonogatari" (Talks of a Western philosopher). *Meiji bunka zenshu,* IV, 429-477.

"Shugiin nisshi" (Proceedings of the *Shugiin*). *Meiji bunka zenshu,* IV, 161-231.

"Sutainshi kogi nikki" (Notes on Stein's lectures). *Meiji bunka zenshu,* IV, 498-613.

Yoshino Sakuzo, ed. *Meiji bunka zenshu* (Collected works on Meiji culture). Vols. III, IV, VII, XIII, XXII. Tokyo, 1928-1930.

B. YEARBOOKS, NEWSPAPERS, SPECIAL STUDIES, AND PERIODICAL ARTICLES IN ENGLISH

Allen, George C. "Concentration of Economic Control in Japan." *Economic Journal,* XLVII (1937), 271-287.

Asakawa Kanichi. "Some Contributions of Feudal Japan to the New Japan." *Journal of Race Development,* III (1912), 1-32.

Ballard, Susan. "A Sketch of the Life of Noboru Watanabe (Kwazan)." *Transactions of the Asiatic Society of Japan,* First Series, XXXII (1905), 1-23.

Borton, Hugh. "Peasant Uprisings in Japan of the Tokugawa Period." *Transactions of the Asiatic Society of Japan, Second Series,* XVI (1938), 1-219.

Clement, Ernest W. "The Mito Civil War." *Transactions of the Asiatic Society of Japan,* First Series, XIX (1891), 393-419.

———. "The Saga and Satsuma Rebellions." *Transactions of the Asiatic Society of Japan,* First Series, L (1922), 13-58.

Colegrove, Kenneth. "The Japanese Cabinet." *American Political Science Review,* XXX (1936), 903-922.

———. "The Japanese Constitution." *American Political Science Review,* XXXI (1937), 1027-1049.

———. "The Japanese Emperor." *American Political Science Review,* XXVI (1932), 642-659, 828-845.

———. "The Japanese Privy Council." *American Political Science Review,* XXV (1931), 589-614, 881-905.

———. "Powers and Functions of the Japanese Diet." *American Political Science Review,* XXVII (1933), 885-898 and XXVIII (1934), 23-39.

Coleman, Horace. "The Life of Yoshida Shoin." *Transactions of the Asiatic Society of Japan,* First Series, XLV (1917), 119-188.

Foreign Affairs Association of Japan, ed. *The Japan Year Book 1938-1939.* Tokyo, 1938.

Greene, D. C. "Osada's Life of Takano Nagahide." *Transactions of the Asiatic Society of Japan,* First Series, XLI (1913), 379-492.

Holtom, D. C. "The Political Philosophy of Modern Shinto." *Transactions of the Asiatic Society of Japan,* First Series, XLIX (1922), 1-325.

Honjo Eijiro. "Changes of Social Classes in the Tokugawa Period." *Kyoto University Economic Review,* III (1928), 56-74.

———. "The Decay of the Samurai Class." *Kyoto University Economic Review,* II (1927), 38-51.

———. "The Importance of 'Goyokin' or Forced Loans in the Meiji Restoration." *Kyoto University Economic Review,* VIII (1933), 18-36.

Bibliography

———. "Short History of Social Problems in Japan Before the Restoration." *Kyoto University Economic Review*, III (1928), 41-85.

Horie Yasuzo. "The Economic Significance of the Meiji Restoration." *Kyoto University Economic Review*, XII (1937), 63-81.

Ike Nobutaka. "Landownership and Taxation in the Westernization of Japan." *The Journal of Economic History*, VII (1947), 160-182.

———. "Triumph of the Peace Party in Japan in 1873." *The Far Eastern Quarterly*, II (1943), 286-295.

Itani Zanichi. "The Economic Causes of the Meiji Restoration." *Transactions of the Asiatic Society of Japan*, Second Series, XVII (1938), 191-207.

The Japan Weekly Mail (Yokohama), 1872-1882.

Kawakami, Karl K. "Political Ideas of Modern Japan." *Studies in Sociology, Economics, Politics, and History*, II (1903), 1-208.

Lay, A. H. "History of the Rise of Political Parties in Japan." *Transactions of the Asiatic Society of Japan*, First Series, XXX (1902), 363-463.

Norman, E. H. "Feudal Background of Japanese Politics." Ninth Conference of the Institute of Pacific Relations, *Secretariat Paper No. 9*, New York, 1945.

Sawada Sho. "Financial Difficulties of the Edo Bakufu." *Harvard Journal of Asiatic Studies*, I (1936), 308-326. Translated by Hugh Borton from *Kokushigaku* (National History), XXII (1935), 1-20.

Smith, Thomas C. "The Introduction of Western Industry in the Last Years of the Tokugawa Period." *Harvard Journal of Asiatic Studies*, XI (1948), 130-152.

Tsuru Shigeto. "Economic Fluctuations in Japan, 1868-1895." *The Review of Economic Statistics*, XXIII (1941), 176-189.

Wilson, Robert A. "The Seitaisho: A Constitutional Experiment" in "Problems of Political Power in Modern Japan, a Symposium." *The Far Eastern Quarterly*, XI (1952), 297-304.

Yanaga Chitoshi. "Theory of the Japanese State." Unpublished Doctoral Dissertation, University of California, 1935.

C. Special Studies and Periodical Articles in Japanese

Hattori Shiso. "Meiji zettaishugi to jiyuminken undo" (Meiji absolutism and the democratic movement). *Nihon rekishigaku koza* (Lectures on Japanese history). Tokyo, 1950.

———. "Tennosei zettaishugi no kakuritsu" (The establishment of imperial absolutism). *Shin nihon shi koza* (New lectures on Japanese history). Tokyo, 1948.

Hirano Yoshitaro. "Meiji ishin ni okeru seijiteki shihai keitai" (The form of political control in the Meiji Restoration). *Nihon shihonshugi hattatsu shi koza* (Lectures on the development of Japanese capitalism). Tokyo, 1933.

Hozumi Yatsukata. "Kempo seitei no yurai" (The origin of the establishment of the constitution). *Meiji bunka zenshu*, V, 419-428.

Ienaga Saburo. "Kyoiku chokugo seiritsu no shisoteki kosatsu" (A study of the ideological background of the imperial rescript on education). *Shigaku zasshi* (History), LVI (1946), 273-291.

Miyajima Seiichiro. "Kokken hensan kigen" (Origins of the compilation of the constitution). *Meiji bunka zenshu*, IV, 341-361.

Osatake Takeki. "Seito shi no issetsu" (An episode in the history of political parties). *Meiji bunka kenkyu*, II (1934), 27-46.

———. "Ito an izen no kempo soan" (Draft constitutions before Ito's draft). *Meiji bunka kenkyu*, I (1934), 2-17.

Uesugi Shigejiro. "Meiji kempo no seiritsu" (The establishment of the Meiji Constitution). *Shin nihon shi koza*. Tokyo, 1948.

Watanabe Kuriyama. "Meiji juyonen seihen ni tsuite" (On the political crisis of 1881). *Meiji bunka kenkyu*, II (1934), 2-27.

D. Books in Western Languages

Allen, George C. *A Short Economic History of Modern Japan 1867-1937*. London, 1946.

Baba Bunyei. *Japan 1853-1864*. Tokyo, 1905. Translated by Ernest Satow from the Japanese.

Black, John R. *Young Japan*. Vol. II. New York, 1883.

Bibliography

Bluntschli, J. K. *The Theory of the State.* Third edition. Oxford, 1901. Translated by D. G. Ritchie, P. E. Matheson, and R. Lodge from the German.
Clement, Ernest W. *Constitutional Imperialism in Japan.* New York, 1916.
Courant, Maurice. *Okoubo.* Paris, 1904.
Fujii Shinichi. *Tenno Seiji* (Imperial government). English edition. Tokyo, 1944.
Griffis, William E. *The Mikado: Institution and Person.* Princeton, 1915.
Gubbins, J. H. *Progress of Japan 1853-1871.* Oxford, 1911.
———. *The Making of Modern Japan.* London, 1922.
Hall, Robert K. *Shushin: The Ethics of a Defeated Nation.* New York, 1949.
Hamada Kengi. *Prince Ito.* Tokyo, 1936.
Hanazono Kanesada. *The Development of Japanese Journalism.* Osaka, 1924.
Holtom, D. C. *The National Faith of Japan.* London, 1938.
Honjo Eijiro. *Economic Theory and History of Japan in the Tokugawa Period.* Tokyo, 1943.
Ijichi Smimasa. *The Life of Marquis Shigenobu Okuma.* Tokyo, 1940.
Ike Nobutaka. *The Beginnings of Political Democracy in Japan.* Baltimore, 1950.
Iwasaki Uichi. *The Working Forces in Japanese Politics.* New York, 1921.
Iyenaga Toyokichi. *The Constitutional Development of Japan 1853-1881.* Baltimore, 1891.
Kawabe Kisaburo. *The Press and Politics in Japan.* Chicago, 1921.
Kiyooka Eiichi. *The Autobiography of Fukuzawa Yukichi.* Authorized edition, Tokyo, 1948.
Kuno Yoshi, S. *Japanese Expansion on the Asiatic Continent.* Vol. II. Berkeley, 1940.
Kuramata Teizo. *A Maker of New Japan: Marquis Ito's Experience.* Nagasaki, 1904.
Matsunami Niichiro. *The Constitution of Japan.* Tokyo, 1930.
———. *The Japanese Constitution and Politics.* Tokyo, 1940.
McLaren, W. W. *A Political History of Japan during the Meiji Era, 1867-1912.* New York, 1916.
Mounsey, Augustus H. *The Satsuma Rebellion.* London, 1879.
Murdoch, James. *A History of Japan.* Vol. III. London, 1926.
Nakamura Katsunoke. *Lord Ii Naosuke and New Japan.* Tokyo, 1909. Translated by Akimoto Shunkichi from the Japanese.
Nakano Tomio. *The Ordinance Power of the Japanese Emperor.* Baltimore, 1923.
Nitobe Inazo, ed. *Western Influence in Modern Japan.* Chicago, 1931.
Norman, E. Herbert. *Japan's Emergence as a Modern State.* New York, 1940.
———. *Soldier and Peasant in Japan: The Origins of Conscription.* New York, 1943.
Okakura Kakuzo. *The Awakening of Japan.* New York, 1905.
Okuma Shigenobu, ed. *Fifty Years of New Japan.* 2 vols. English edition edited by Marcus B. Huish. London, 1910.
Pooley, A. M. *Japan at the Crossroads.* New York, 1917.
Quigley, Harold S. *Japanese Government and Politics.* New York, 1932.
Reischauer, Robert K. *Japan: Government-Politics.* New York, 1939.
Sansom, Sir George B. *Japan, A Short Cultural History.* Revised edition. New York, 1943.
———. *Japan in World History.* New York, 1951.
———. *The Western World and Japan.* New York, 1950.
Sato Hiroshi. *Democracy and the Japanese Government.* New York, 1920.
Stead, Alfred, ed. *Japan by the Japanese.* London, 1904.
Takekoshi Yosaburo. *The Economic Aspects of the History of the Civilization of Japan.* Vols. II and III. London and New York, 1930.
———. *Prince Saionji.* Kyoto, 1933.
Takizawa Matsuyo. *The Penetration of Money Economy in Japan.* New York, 1927.
Uyehara, George E. *The Political Development of Japan 1867-1909.* London, 1910.
Yanaga Chitoshi. *Japan Since Perry.* New York, 1949.

E. Books in Japanese

Asai Kiyoshi. *Meiji rikken shiso ni okeru eikoku gikai seido no eikyo* (The influence of the English parliamentary system on Meiji constitutional thought). Tokyo, 1935.
———. *Genroin no kempo hensan temmatsu* (An account of the compilation of the draft constitutions by the *Genroin*). Tokyo, 1946.

Bibliography

Fujii Jintaro. *Nihon kempo seitei shi* (History of the establishment of the Japanese constitution). Tokyo, 1929.

Fujii Jintaro and Moriya Hidesuke. *Sogo nihon shi taikei: Meiji jidai shi* (A synthesis of Japanese history: the Meiji period). Revised edtion. Tokyo, 1940.

Fujii Shinichi. *Teikoku kempo to Kaneko haku* (The imperial constitution and Count Kaneko). Tokyo, 1942.

Ishin Shiryo Hensan Jimmukyoku. *Ishin shi* (History of the restoration). Vol. V. Tokyo, 1939-1941.

Ito Hirobumi den (The biography of Ito Hirobumi). Vol. II. Tokyo, 1940. Published by the Shunbo Ko Tsuisho Kai.

Kikuta Sadao. *Seikan ron no shinso to sono eikyo* (The truth about the Korean war controversy and its influence). Tokyo, 1941.

Kiyomizu Shin. *Dokuo ni okeru Ito Hirobumi no kempo torishirabe to nihon kempo* (Ito Hirobumi's constitutional investigation in Germany and the Japanese constitution). Tokyo, 1935.

Meiji shiyo (Epitome of Meiji history). Tokyo Imperial University edition, Tokyo, 1933.

Nakamura Kikuo. *Nihon kindaika to Fukuzawa Yukichi* (Fukuzawa Yukichi and the modernization of Japan). Second edition. Tokyo, 1950.

Oka Yoshitake. *Kindai nihon no keisei* (The formation of modern Japan). Tokyo, 1947.

Osatake Takeki. *Ishin zengo ni okeru rikken shiso* (Constitutional thought before and after the restoration). 2 vols. Tokyo, 1929.

———. *Nihon kensei shi* (History of Japanese constitutional government). Tokyo, 1930.

———. *Nihon kensei shi taiko* (An outline of Japanese constitutional history). 2 vols. Tokyo, 1938.

———. *Meiji seiji shi tembyo* (Sketches on Meiji political history). Tokyo, 1938.

Otsu Junichiro. *Dai nihon kensei shi* (History of constitutional government in Japan). Vol. II. Tokyo, 1929.

Ozaki Yukio. *Nihon kensei shi o kataru* (On the history of constitutional government in Japan). Tokyo, 1938.

Sato Kiyokatsu. *Dai nihon seiji shiso shi* (History of Japanese political thought). Vol. II. Tokyo, 1939.

Shibuzawa Eiichi. *Tokugawa Keiki ko den* (The biography of Prince Tokugawa Keiki). Vol. IV. Tokyo, 1917.

Suzuki Yasuzo. *Kempo no rekishiteki kenkyu* (Historical studies on the constitution). Tokyo, 1934.

———. *Nihon kempo shi kenkyu* (Studies in Japanese constitutional history). Tokyo, 1935.

———. *Nihon kensei shi gaisetsu* (Outline of the history of Japanese constitutional government). Tokyo, 1941.

———. *Meiji shonen no rikken shiso* (Constitutional thought in the early years of the Meiji era). Tokyo, 1938.

Toyama Shigeki. *Meiji ishin shi* (History of the Meiji Restoration). Tokyo, 1951.

Tokutomi Iichiro. *Koshaku Yamagata Aritomo den* (Biography of Prince Yamagata Aritomo). Vol. II. Tokyo, 1939.

Watanabe Ikujiro. *Meiji tenno to rikken seiji* (The Emperor Meiji and constitutional government). Tokyo, 1937.

———. *Nihon kempo seitei shi ko* (Lectures on the history of the establishment of the Japanese constitution). Tokyo, 1939.

Yamada Seitaro. *Nihon shihonshugi bunseki* (An analysis of Japanese capitalism). Tokyo, 1935.

Appendix I

Constitution Ordered to be Drafted by Kido Koin between 1872 and 1874

Chapter I: The National Boundaries

Article I. Japan consists of the various islands and prefectures belonging to the Japanese Empire at present.

Article II. The boundaries of these areas shall not be changed except by the force of law (see below).

Chapter II: The Rights and Duties of the People

Article III. Whether a person acquires nationality and becomes a Japanese subject or divests himself of that status shall be decided after decision by both Bureaus of the Government.

Article IV. Japanese subjects are either nobles (*kazoku*) or commoners. Both are henceforth free to choose their occupations.

Article V. The land of Japan shall be owned by Japanese subjects.

Article VI. Regardless of special standing based on lineage, all commoners and nobles are entirely equal before the laws of the land. Moreover, the abuses of transmitting public offices by heredity shall be removed so that all people may have the right to hold office according to their ability.

Article VII. The people are free to change their residence within the country (freedom to move about at will) in accordance with the change of residence law.

Article VIII. The natural rights of each person shall be protected. Accordingly, no one may be brought to trial forcibly without due process of law; nor may anyone be refused a court trial against his wishes or against his interests.

Article IX. Even in the case of a pilferer or thief, he may not be arrested arbitrarily unless the crime is committed on the spot. Persons under suspicion may be arrested only by order of a judge according to due process of law.

Article X. Punishments shall be judicial decisions in accordance with the criminal code, and arbitrary vengeance shall be strictly prohibited. Unless it is an exceptional case (creation of wealth through counterfeiting), the confiscation of the family wealth of a criminal is henceforth abolished.

Article XI. The authorities who try cases and give verdicts shall be equal and the same for both nobles and commoners.

Article XII. In unavoidable circumstances, entry into a private house, search and seizure, and examination of family property shall be conducted according to due process of law. Otherwise, forceful entry into a private residence is strictly prohibited.

Article XIII. Private property may never be forcibly seized. If, however, it is necessary to take such property for public use, suitable compensation shall be paid for the loss incurred.

Appendix I

Article XIV. According to the law of marriage, when a couple plans to marry, it must notify a judge. After his examination, it may go through with the marriage ceremony.

Article XV. Without distinction between nobles and commoners, all Japanese are entitled to marry one husband or one wife. In short, bigamy is not permitted.

Article XVI. Marriages between nobles and commoners, of course, may be made according to the wishes of each. When a girl born into a noble family marries into a commoner family, she shall lose the title of noble from the day of the marriage. When a girl of the commoner class marries into a noble family, the opposite is true. (In consideration of the house laws of the Imperial and Princely Families, their royal positions must be respected.)

Article XVII. With the exception of the Imperial and Princely Families, even though one has no children, the practice of taking another's child and raising it as an adopted son is strictly forbidden from this day on.

Article XVIII. In Japan, Buddhism is the religion in which we principally have faith. Consequently, we shall prohibit belief in Christianity and other religions for the time being.

Article XIX. Boys and girls of Japan, without distinction between nobles and commoners, shall enter schools established by the central, prefectural, and district Governments and pursue an elementary education as best possible. For both boys and girls the age of matriculation is eight years old. Fathers and guardians of children who are nine and have not entered school shall be disciplined suitably according to the regulations of the Department of Education.

Article XX. Individuals and groups are free to establish private schools, and boys and girls may enter public or private schools according to their own convenience and wishes. In short, there shall be no difference at all in the character of their schooling because it is public or private.

Article XXI. Whether in a public or private school, the curriculum and methods of education shall be the same as far as possible throughout the entire land. A person wishing to found a school must formulate rules of instruction and show them to the Department of Education. Then, after obtaining approval, he may open his school.

Article XXII. The construction and maintenance expenses of schools shall be provided through the joint efforts of the Governments of the prefectures, districts, and groups of villages *(kumi)* according to the regulations of the Department of Education. However, if the *kumi* is impoverished, the various expenses shall be paid by the Government. In the case of schools for the poor, the Government shall not only pay the construction and maintenance expenses, but students shall be able to attend at cost.

Article XXIII. Public school teachers shall earn government salaries like other officials. In the matter of rank, they shall be regarded as officials.

Appendix I

Article XXIV. Although everyone is free to express his own views by means of speech, writing, printing, etc., anyone who slanders the Government and fellow men, disturbs customs, arouses the people with seditious ideas, and leads them into dangerous ways, shall not escape punishment according to law.

Article XXV. The publisher of a newspaper or magazine shall submit a copy of his publication to the Police Board before making it public and ask permission to sell. There must be an indication of his responsibility for observations and reports by recording his full name at the beginning and end of the publication. The same shall apply to school texts. It is strictly forbidden to sell publications without the name of the author.

Article XXVI. Whether noble or commoner, all citizens of Japan are liable for military service. The kind and length of service shall be decided by the regulations of the Army and Navy. (Until these are established, we shall continue as at present.) When officers or soldiers desert or commit a crime, they shall be disciplined according to military regulations.

Article XXVII. Without distinction between nobles or commoners, all residents of Japan shall pay suitable taxes according to the law of taxation. Europeans and Americans living in foreign settlements shall be a special case. Foreign diplomatic representatives shall be in the same category.

Article XXVIII. People are free to submit petitions and complaints to the various administrative Departments and Parliament. However, unsigned petitions and complaints shall not be accepted. Therefore, the complaint box is henceforth abolished.

Article XXIX. People are free to assemble together at one place provided they are unarmed and to form associations if they are not contrary to law. If people hold meetings on thoroughfares or out of doors, they shall inform the police three days in advance and ask for permission.

Article XXX. In time of peace, mail may not be opened even by order of the Government. On the other hand, in time of war or in cases of emergency in the investigation of crimes, suspicious letters, although they may be private, may be opened in accordance with legal restrictions.

Chapter III: The Affairs of State

Article XXXI. All the articles of the Constitution are rules agreed upon between the Emperor and the people. Thus, even the policies of the Emperor and his officials shall be regarded as the result of harmony existing between the sovereign and his people, unless such policies are actually in violation of the purposes of laws.

Article XXXII. The power to enact laws is basically the prerogative of the Emperor and Parliament. The Emperor, however, settles the discussion which enacts laws and the Representatives participate in the discussion.

Appendix I

Article XXXIII. The various laws and provisional edicts shall be promulgated when the Imperial Seal has been affixed to them.

Article XXXIV. The authority to conduct the administration in conformance with the provisions of the Constitution resides entirely in the Emperor.

Article XXXV. The authority to establish legal principles and judge crimes resides entirely in the Courts.

Chapter IV A: The Powers of the Emperor

Article XXXVI. The Emperor is sacred and inviolable, and his Ministers shall always observe their responsibility to him. (When a complaint is brought against a Minister by Members of Parliament, if he puts down the circumstances clearly in writing, he may escape punishment. However, when his conduct is excessive and there is no truth to his explanation, the offender shall be dismissed from office. This is what "responsibility" means.)

Article XXXVII. The Emperor has the power to approve laws and issue edicts. When for some reason a law is not carried out or there is some obstacle, this situation may be remedied by an Imperial emergency edict. However, even Imperial orders as well as regular Imperial edicts shall never be promulgated without a Minister's countersignature; moreover, the Minister who has signed shall bear responsibility for it.

XXXVIII. The Emperor alone has the power to appoint and dismiss Ministers and other administrative and military officials and to confer honors. However, this rule does not apply to those persons whose position has been established by special law, i.e., election of the heads of *kumi*. Aside from the Emperor, no one may hold a military and civil post at the same time, even by order of the Emperor, i.e., the Ministers of the Army and the Navy must be appointed from among military officers, and those who hold civil administrative posts must be appointed from among the non-military.

XXXIX. The Emperor is Commander-in-Chief of the Army and Navy. General military powers, especially decisions regarding war and peace and the conclusion of alliances, are the powers of the Emperor alone. The conclusion of treaties of amity and trade with other nations is also among the powers of the Emperor. Treaties of amity and commerce shall be promulgated after they are signed; and the meaning of the edict and of the signed treaty must not disagree in the slightest.

Article XL. The Emperor has the power to mitigate criminal sentences after an investigation (to commute execution to exile or life in prison to a term sentence) and to terminate criminal investigations (end the period in which the conduct of an arrested suspect is investigated). After a charge against a Minister is judged in Court, no one, not even the Emperor, may reduce the punishment without the approval of Parliament, which inaugurated the suit.

Appendix I

Article XLI. The Emperor has the power to convoke and close Parliament (and to dissolve Parliament in an emergency). However, when Parliament is dissolved, a completely new Parliament shall be selected within six months or 180 days.

Article XLI A. In addition to the several Ministers and Parliamentary Representatives, the Emperor shall assemble elder statesmen in a Cabinet. When there are important administrative problems, he shall call them together and ask their advice.

Article XLII. The Emperor has the power to award prizes (medals for meritorious service) and titles of nobility *(kazoku)*. However, the nobles shall have no special rank.

Article XLIII. The Emperor has the power to mint money for circulation (gold or silver for public use).

Article XLIV. Each year the Imperial expenditures shall be decided by law and paid out of tax revenues.

Article XLV. The Emperor may not become the sovereign of another country without the consent of Parliament.

Article XLVI. The accession to the Throne shall be limited to the line of Emperor Jimmu. A son of the Emperor, particularly the eldest son, shall succeed to the Throne. When the Emperor dies and there is no direct heir, the Ministers or the Members of Parliament in council shall elect a new Emperor from among the four Imperial Families.

Article XLVII. The Emperor attains majority at eighteen years of age (or 216 months) and consequently may ascend the Throne. When the Emperor is not yet eighteen years old, a Regent shall be chosen from among the members of the Imperial Family by the Ministers and Parliament. The provisions of this Constitution may not be changed during the period of the Regency.

Article XLVIII. When ascending the Throne, the Emperor shall swear before an assemblage of Parliamentary Representatives that he shall govern according to the articles of the Constitution and the laws. When a member of the Imperial Family becomes Regent, he shall swear the same thing.

Article XLIX. When the Emperor dies or is unable to administer the affairs of State because of a serious illness, the Crown Prince shall of course ascend the Throne. When the Crown Prince is not yet eighteen years old, the members of the Imperial Family who are eligible for the Regency shall be summoned, and the process of selecting one of them to become Regent shall be carried out.

Article L. When the Emperor and the Princes-of-the Blood are minors, the Ministers and Parliamentary Representatives shall manage the affairs of State jointly until the Emperor attains majority.

Article LI. The private property (forests, lands, money, palaces, buildings, etc.) of the Imperial Family shall be determined by law. (The private property of the Imperial Family shall be provided for separately.)

Appendix I

Chapter IV B: The Rights and Duties of Ministers

Article LII. A member of the Imperial Family and a person who is not a Japanese subject may not hold the office of Minister.

Article LIII. Even if a Minister appears to have committed an offense against the Government, unless there is substantial evidence presented by the Members of Parliament and a complaint presented to the Emperor, he may not be dismissed from office improperly because of public censure.

Article LIV. The conditions of ministerial responsibility, complaints of the offenses of Ministers, methods of judgment, and the manner of punishment shall be determined separately by law.

Article LV. When a Minister is seriously ill or is traveling with official permission, the Vice-Minister shall represent him. During this period, the Vice-Minister shall be held responsible for violations of administrative regulations.

Article LVI. The Ministers have the duty to enable the Emperor to manage the administration tranquilly in accordance with the provisions of the Constitution and the laws. Among the Ministers, there shall be a Prime Minister *(Dajodaijin)* and a Deputy Prime Minister.

Chapter IV C: The Senate *(Genroin)*

Article LVII. As for the duties of the *Genroin,* it shall assist the Emperor and act as his adviser in accordance with the provisions of the Constitution and the laws. When a Minister violates a constitutional provision administratively or when he breaks a law, the *Genroin* has the right to censure him.

Article LVIII. The Emperor has the power to appoint persons to this advisory post and to raise their rank. According to circumstances, he may appoint a Minister to the *Genroin* or restore him to a ministry. The members of the *Genroin,* however, shall be chosen by the Emperor from among officials of *chokunin* rank who have rendered distinguished service in the past; and unless they pay annual taxes of 210 yen, they are ineligible for office.

Article LIX. The Members of the *Genroin,* aside from a stipend granted by the Emperor, shall not be entitled to a monthly salary.

Chapter IV D: The Rights of Parliament [Lower House]

Article LVII A. The elected Members of Parliament shall represent the people of Japan. They shall meet and discuss because the affairs of State are not the concern of the Emperor alone but are also of interest to the people. Although the selected Representatives shall be chosen from the prefectures, when they are assembled in session and pitted against the Government, each shall be aware that he represents the people of Japan as a whole and not the narrow interests of his prefecture.

Appendix I

Article LVIII A. Although the principal duty of the Representatives shall be to take part in discussions formulating legislation, both Parliament and the Government shall have the right to initiate legislation. Parliament may also audit the expenditures and receipts of the Government annually.

Article LIX A. The Representatives, when in session, shall express their views and shall not be afraid to speak their minds. The people shall be permitted to attend and listen. However, the President of Parliament shall have the right to institute secret sessions according to the circumstances. When it is time to make a decision regarding legislation, the President of Parliament shall put the question to the Members, and the matter shall be decided by vote. When a bill is drafted in Parliament or when a bill is closely examined, such business shall be dealt with by a committee selected from among the Members of Parliament.

Article LX. Persons are eligible for membership in Parliament if they have been elected to the posts of Prefectural Governor or Chief Justice. They shall be replaced every three years. At this interval, Representatives shall be newly selected from among the Governors and Chief Justices. The Court Nobility shall participate in Parliament for life. The method by which they shall be selected shall be determined by a separate law.

Article LX A. Although Parliamentary Representatives shall be elected by the people, for a time, the Emperor shall appoint them from among the Prefectural Governors and Chief Justices. Moreover, twenty-nine Court Nobles shall be permanent members without election.

Article LXI. No one may be a Member of Parliament unless he is a Japanese subject, pays sixty yen in taxes annually, and is thirty years old. Anyone who has been punished for a crime is ineligible.

Article LXII. When the Members of Parliament convene for the first time, they shall reciprocally question each other's qualifications (citizenship, age, past conduct, etc.). Thereupon, they shall select a President and Vice-President. However, while the Members of Parliament have the right to nominate these officers, the power of appointment rests with the Emperor. Thus, when Parliament chooses these officers, it shall submit the names of three candidates to the Emperor without making distinction according to President or Vice-President. The Emperor shall consider the three candidates, and if he thinks that they are not suitable, he shall choose others and appoint them.

Article LXIII. When a Member of Parliament, who has not completed his three year term becomes an administrative official by order of the Emperor, he shall lose his parliamentary title and shall no longer be able to participate in parliamentary proceedings. Administrative officials (even though they are in the Departments of Justice or Education), who are selected as Members of Parliament, may not return to their former posts within the period of their membership. Although Governors and Chief Justices have attended the first session of Parliament, they may retain their

Appendix I

original positions and upon the closing of Parliament return to their prefectural posts and take up their original offices.

Article LXIV. When all the Members of Parliament are to be replaced in some emergency, former Members shall once again be selected. When all the Members are replaced at the end of their term, the same holds true. When a Governor of Chief Justice is excused from serving as a Member of Parliament, the Emperor shall select the deputy to the Governor or Chief Justice, or an administrative official from a Department to fill the vacancy.

Article LXV. Parliament shall meet in Tokyo. The annual convocation date shall be the twentieth day of the twelfth month. After a session of fifty days, Parliament shall be closed. On the opening and closing days, the Emperor shall be present in the hall and conduct the ceremonies. If, for some reason, the Emperor cannot open or close Parliament, a Prince or Minister who knows the sentiments of the Emperor shall conduct the ceremonies on that day.

Artilce LXVI. When a Minister or Vice-Minister commits an offense against the Government, first Parliament shall insist that he be held responsible. When it is clear that his explanation is unreliable or there has been criminal intent, Parliament shall ascertain the circumstances and make a complaint to the Emperor. When there is a written complaint from the people regarding the misconduct of a Minister or Vice-Minister and Parliament agrees with the charge, Parliament shall urge in writing that he be held responsible. However, if a number of complaints are addressed to only one member, Parliament shall not give approval to them.

Article LXVII. With the exception of those members who are Court Nobles, all the elected Representatives shall receive from the Government their traveling expenses to and from Tokyo and *per diem* allowances while in Tokyo. However, they shall not receive salaries additional to their regular monthly salaries. Moreover, the Court Nobles shall not receive salaries, traveling expenses, etc.

Article LXVIII. Although Representatives break laws during the fifty days of Parliament's session, they may not be arrested or tried in court. However, when someone is found to have committed an act of violence, this provision does not apply.

Chapter IV E: Provisions for Local Government

Article LXIX. The local areas of Japan are divided into *do* (circuits), *ken* (prefectures), *gun* (districts), and *kumi* (village circles). The fixed limits of the authority of appointed officials like Prefectural Governors and heads of *kumi* shall be decided separately by law.
(a) When broad discussion is necessary on some matter relative to the *do, ken, gun,* or *kumi,* in which the people are interested, a conference may be called to make the decision. However, when there is need for such a

Appendix I

meeting, the people shall first inform the Government of the circumstances and request permission before the meeting is held.

(b) The authority to appoint Prefectural Governors, etc., resides in the Emperor; however, the *kumi* heads shall be elected by the residents of the *kumi*.

(c) The local affairs of the *kumi* shall be managed and decided by the residents of the *kumi*. Districts with more than 300 residents shall provide their own constables (several *kumi* joining together) in accordance with the police laws.

(d) Prefectural Governors, etc., and heads of *kumi* shall account each year for receipts and expenditures in their jurisdictions and report these to the Government.

Chapter IV F: Legal Matters

Article LXX. Jurisdiction over public and private suits resides in the general Courts. The management of legal affairs shall be decided by law; moreover, judges shall render decisions carefully without considering their own personal feelings or those of others. The judgment of suits and determination of punishments shall be decided according to due process of law, and the reasons for penalties and punishments shall be demonstrated. All penalties and punishments shall be administered in the name of the Emperor.

Article LXXI. Courts shall be divided into three groups: 1st, 2nd, and 3rd. (There shall be no distinction between public and private suits.) In each *do,* there shall be a 2nd class Court, and in each *gun* a 1st class Court. As for 3rd class Courts, there shall be only one—in Tokyo. Military and Commercial Courts and matters pertaining to them shall be determined separately by law.

Article LXXII. Ordinary trials shall be held publicly in Court. However, when a trial concerns debauchery or will arouse the feelings of those in attendance, it shall be made public but tried in closed session.

Article LXXIII. Judges shall pass sentence. The Emperor shall select persons expert in the legal system and in law and place them in these offices. They shall administer judicial affairs with full power. Once judges are appointed to their positions, they shall be promoted gradually; and unless they violate laws or legal regulations, they may continue in office for life. Judges shall confine their administration to the affairs of justice and may not hold other offices. However, if they are selected as Parliamentary Representatives, they shall be exceptions to this rule.

Article LXXIV. The limits of judicial power and general legal regulations shall be decided by law.

Article LXXV. Disputes that arise between administrative and judicial officials shall be settled according to the procedure provided for in Article LIV.

Appendix I

Article LXXVI. When a judge violates the limits of judicial power and breaks regulations, anyone with knowledge of this shall file a complaint immediately.

Article LXXVII. When a judge dies after two years in office, the Government shall pay an allowance to his wife and children according to judicial regulations.

Chapter IV G: Finance

Article LXXVIII. Yearly revenues and expenditures shall be estimated beforehand by the Department of Finance, and each Minister shall present his Department estimate to Parliament. The annual expenditures of the Government shall be decided by law.

Article LXXIX. As for the annual expenditures of each Department, the Minister shall briefly record the nature of its expenditures and show them to Parliament. When Parliament has doubts regarding the expenditures, the Minister may not refuse to have them investigated.

Article LXXX. When under extreme circumstances expenditures exceed their limit in a given year, the Government shall give clear proof of the actual circumstances when Parliament reconvenes.

Article LXXXI. Public taxes provided for in the tax laws shall be collected each year by the Department of Finance. When it becomes necessary to levy new taxes, Parliament, if it approves, shall enact a new tax law.

Article LXXXII. Although annual expenditures in the *do, ken,* and *gun* are under their jurisdiction, Governors may not provide for their expenditures by levying taxes according to their own will. For the necessary expenses of administration each Governor within his own jurisdiction shall convene an assembly to determine the amount of taxes annually by a tax law.

Article LXXXIII. Commissions (legal fees, notarizations, passport taxes, etc.) shall be paid by each Bureau according to law.

Article LXXXIV. Matters concerning the national debt and the liability of the Government for it shall be disposed of by law on each occasion.

Article LXXXV. The payment of new allowances shall be abolished. Whenever someone is to be paid a prize for some exceptional, meritorious service, it shall be decided by law.

Chapter V: Concerning Officials

Article LXXXVI. The appointment and dismissal of officials as well as allowances to their wives and children, other than those of the judiciary, shall be decided by law. Administrative officials shall not be dismissed improperly for personal reasons, unless their conduct and aims are harmful to the purposes of the Government.

Appendix I

Article LXXXVII. Persons remaining in office prior to the promulgation of the Constitution shall be rewarded under special administrative provisions of the personnel regulations.

Article LXXXVIII. Members of Parliament who are administrative officials, although they do not work in their original posts, shall receive their salaries as before.

Chapter VI: General Provisions

Article LXXXIX. When emergency or general matters are pressing and Parliament is not in session, the Ministers accepting joint responsibility shall issue an extra proclamation according to the circumstances. Although this may relieve the emergency and take the place of law, when Parliament reconvenes, the Government shall explain the circumstances to it and if necessary submit a written report.

Article XC. Laws and emergency proclamations by the *do, ken,* and *gun* Governments shall be announced in the manner of laws (with the countersignature of the Governor). Otherwise, they shall not take effect.

Article XCI. Instructions now in force shall remain effective so long as they do not conflict with these articles.

Article XCII. Officials now in office shall continue to serve until the limits of their authority are decided by law and criteria of their service are regulated.

Article XCIII. Parliamentary Representatives and administrative officials will present a written oath to the Emperor to serve him loyally, sincerely, and faithfully.

Article XCIV. Only in time of war, the provisions of Articles VIII, IX, XII, XXIII, XXIV, XXV, XXVIII, XXIX, and XXX may be suspended by law in whole or in part.

Chapter VII: Amendment of the Constitution

Article XCV. Whenever these articles are not suited to the process of Government, the executive or Parliament may provide reasons and it shall be decided by discussion. If both Houses are in agreement, the amendment may be made.

Appendix II

Okubo Toshimichi's Opinion on Constitutional Government 1873

In the world, people who discuss the systems of government talk in terms of monarchy and democracy. Japan cannot yet adopt democracy, and Japan cannot yet discard monarchy. Indeed, monarchy is rooted in the very founding of our nation. It is the first principle of our government. It is the supreme type of government. If we do not establish monarchy firmly, how can we build the nation? How can we administer the affairs of state?

Democracy seeks to work for the common welfare of the people. It does not seek to make the nation the realm of any one person. Universally, it signifies freedom of the people. It is a system of government perfected according to the laws of nature, but it does not ignore the principles of administration by law and the responsibility of officials. At present, it is the system of government in the United States, Switzerland, and South America. This system of government can be put into operation when new nations are founded or by new nations of immigrants, but it cannot be applied to a people who are accustomed to long-standing practices based on old ways. Switzerland is a naturally protected, rich land. The attitude of this single country affects the situation in the whole of Europe. Therefore the various nations of Europe struggle against and check each other from harboring evil ambitions against that country. The United States is hardly one hundred years old. In the beginning, it suffered the oppression of monarchy, and its people have built their nation upon the principle of democracy. In other countries this system of government was instituted because they were new nations and new peoples. However, this system is not free from abuses. With the establishment of political parties, which gradually grow larger, political deterioration and disintegration set in. In the past, the democracy of France was said to be much more brutal and cruel than French absolute monarchy. This is a case where name and reality clash. One cannot say that democracy is the best system of government.

In the case of monarchy, when the people are unenlightened, rule based upon a contract is impossible. The person who more or less excels in ability wields power; and he rules by limiting freedom and restricting natural justice. This is surely the best method of government applicable to this temporary situation. However, even though the ruler is wise and his advisers able and thus the people do not suffer misfortune nor the nation defeat, there are still shortcomings in this type of government. It cannot escape a lack of stability in the execution of its domestic and foreign policies. If the day comes that a tyrant and corrupt officials seize power arbitrarily and exercise the power of life and death at their whim, popular resentment will very often arise to reproach the person of the ruler, resulting in dethronement or usurpation. Generally, when laws are artificial and not based on natural order, government cannot be maintained for long, given

Appendix II

the conditions of the times and the feelings of the people. Lessons may be learned from Cromwell in England and the revolution in eighteenth century France. Although democracy and monarchy differ as systems of government, generally both are established according to the conditions, customs, and feelings of the people of the land. One should not simply set out to establish them by will. On the other hand, a nation cannot hold to the same kind of government just because it is old. The Russian system of government cannot be put into operation in England; and the English system of government cannot be utilized in the United States. The systems of the United States, England, or Russia cannot be implemented in Japan.

In view of this, we must establish a system of government in our country that is consistent with our conditions, customs, and tendencies. Since the Meiji Restoration, we have endeavored to study and learn from the rest of the world, and to make Japan superior to all nations. Our government, however, has retained the system of monarchy that is traditional to the country, and it is rightfully applicable today. Our country occupies a strategic position in world navigation, and its customs include the traits to make progress. Our people are already under the influence of Europe and America, and we are already partially modernized. In the future, we will not be able to keep the same kind of government.

In this case, shall the government become a government of the people? No! Although, in the autumn of 1871, a decree abolishing the *han* was promulgated and an order establishing the prefectural system was issued so that there would be consistency in government instructions, for almost one thousand years, the people have been accustomed to the oppressive feudal system and its unfortunate practices. Given the customs and feelings of the people, how can the country be adjusted to new institutions? Democracy, of course, cannot be established in Japan, and the old monarchy can no longer be maintained. We must develop a political system that conforms to the customs, feelings, and conditions of our nation. We must decide on a fixed statute for the state, that is, a system of constitutional monarchy.

England is an island nation in Europe with a land area of 20,500 square *ri* and a population of over 32,000,000. The Norman Conquest was just a little more than 800 years ago, and since that time, England has spread its power overseas and brought many lands under its control. The nation is so prosperous today because it has a good government under which every one of its 32,000,000 people exerts himself for the independence of his country in order to realize his rights, while the rulers develop the ability and powers of the people.

Japan too is an island nation in Asia. Its land area is 23,000 square *ri*, and its population is over 31,000,000. It has been a thousand years since the nation had a reform in the reign of the Emperor Tenchi, and there is nothing comparable to the prosperity of England. This is because, of the more than 31,000,000 people, those who revere the Emperor and love the

Appendix II

country are one in ten thousand, and under the system of government, ability is restricted and rights are limited. This is clear proof of the fact that a nation can rise or decline according to the ablity of the people who support it and to the system of government which will nourish such ability.

Since our forefathers founded the nation, Japan has not had a government that did not include the people; nor have we maintained the country without monarchy. Constitutional monarchy is a joint government of the ruler and the people; it is a limited monarchy. It seeks to determine the powers of the monarch and the people in an equitable fashion. Both the monarch and the people must not think only of their own interests. In general, when people associate with one another, there is competition. When the monarch and the people are thrown together, there is competition between them. And when the monarch and the people struggle, justice must settle the dispute. Where ultimate power is vested in the ruler, the system is monarchy. Where it is vested in the people, it is democracy. Where it is vested in both the ruler and the people, it is limited monarchy. In order to protect and extend the rights and powers of both the ruler and the people, with their consent, an unremovable constitution is established. All state affairs are conducted according to the constitution, which is the supreme power in the land. Once this system of government is established, officials will not conduct the administration by their own arbitrary judgment. In the operation of government there will be careful conformance to regulations, and there will not be the evil inconsistency. When the people and the government are united, modernization will not be fruitless. This shall be the foundation of our nation and the basis of our government. All our people, now in various walks of life, must be sure to recognize this.

Although this be the case, let me ask—Can we adopt this proposal and lessen the supreme power of the Emperor? The answer is—No! The more the outward appearance of the power of the Emperor is strengthened, the less his actual power will be. Thus, in the days when Taira Masakado held the reins of power, the Emperor lived in a palace, maintained pomp and ceremony, and was worshipped by the people. However, he had little power. When the Emperor actually rules, the people will respect him and know him to be a man after all. That the Emperor partially loses his outward power and the people day by day become more enlightened is the result of nature's power which man cannot expect to check. If we seek to strengthen his outward power without taking this into consideration, although the Emperor reigns, he will be powerless. This will be no different than in the old days of Taira Masakado, and the position of the Emperor will be in peril. Thus, the basic law which will determine the powers of the Emperor and limit the powers of the people must be based on a profound love of the nation. It must maintain the Emperor's position for all ages to come and make the people keep their natural order.

Appendix II

Nothing can be more important today than discussion concerning our system of government, However, we should not be in too great haste. We should discuss the matter orderly as Japanese. We must not imitate the limited monarchies of the various nations of Europe. Our country has a code of an unbroken imperial line, and the people have a degree of modernization. Having considered the advantages and disadvantages to the Emperor and the people, I think we should establish a constitution.

In the form of its government, each nation adheres to its old customs and the feelings of its people. Although monarchical absolutism, limited monarchy, and republicanism differ, the system of government of each does not act resolutely in deciding and implementing the affairs of state unless there is some firm, independent power. Many persons offer opinions, and in the end each person advocates his own opinion without firm foundation. Thus, each system of government lacks direction in the beginning and loses order in administration. When each wishes to advocate, it retreats; and when each wishes to hurry, it remains at ease. The administration becomes stagnant, and it lacks stability.

Among the three kinds of government, monarchial absolutism means a system which has no fixed laws. The will of the monarch is national law, and there are no limits to the power of the ruler. Limited monarchy follows traditional precedents, and it establishes the boundaries of power between the ruler and the people. It establishes law, and the ruler conducts the administration according to it. Republicanism, or more properly, government by the people, exerts its power for the people and establishes a constitution. It is a system of government under which elected representatives conduct the administration according to a constitution. However, in each system, there is some core of firm and independent power to decide and administer the affairs of state. In monarchical absolutism, only the ruler's will is regarded as inviolable. In countries where there is limited monarchy or republicanism, a fixed constitution and laws are regarded as unshakable. If we consider our political system, it is something which combines the good points of the above three systems. Yet, although it seems well adapted to our national customs and well suited to the times, in reality, it is not completely satisfactory. Why is this so? He who issues decrees and he who has actual power are not the same. To take the human body for example, when arms and legs go in different directions, doing what they like and running where they like, there is no center for coördination and coöperation. Thus, having given careful attention to this and having assessed present trends, I put forward the following proposal:

* * * *

1. Organization of the *Dajokan*

    Three Bureaus *(Seiin, Sain,* and *Uin)* and one Board (Ceremonies) constitute the *Dajokan*.

Appendix II

Seiin. The Emperor attends. The *Dajodaijin* assists the Emperor and manages the affairs of state. He reports memorials to the throne and affixes seals of imperial approval upon them. He also signs imperial rescripts and affixes a seal upon them. He presides over the *Uin.* The *Sadaijin,* in official duties, follows the *Dajodaijin.* When the *Dajodaijin* is absent, he may assume his duties. In the *Uin,* together with the Councillors *(Sangi),* he shares responsibility for settling the affairs of state. The *Seiin* has a Secretariat.

Sain. A chairman is selected from the *Sadaijin, Udaijin,* and the Councillors. It is responsble for the discussion of laws.

Uin. The *Dajodaijin* is chairman. With the Councillors, he discusses and settles the affairs of state.

Shikiburyo (Board of Ceremonies).

2. *Seiin.* The *Seiin,* in the presence of the Emperor, decides the affairs of state. The *Dajodaijin, Sadaijin,* and *Udaijin* assist the Emperor. The *Seiin* promotes the general administration. Government regulations and special imperial orders are promulgated by the *Seiin* under the signature of the *Dajodaijin.* Matters concerning the division or amalgamation of administrative Departments and Bureaus are reported to the Emperor after discussion by the *Uin.* If he approves, orders are promulgated by the *Seiin.* The appointment and dismissal of officials of *chokunin* rank, although a decision of the Emperor, is discussed by the *Uin* and then reported to the throne by the *Dajodaijin.* The appointment and dismissal of officials of *sonin* rank, although reported to the throne by the head official concerned, is first discussed by the *Uin* and falls under the final jurisdiction of the *Dajodaijin.* The appointment and dismissal of officials of *hanin* rank in the *Seiin* is reported by the official concerned and falls under the jurisdiction of the Secretariat.

When it has been decided that there seems to have been a miscarriage of justice in a serious panel case, a judicial officer reports the circumstances; and after deliberation by the *Uin,* the *Dajodaijin* reports it to the throne. After imperial sanction is obtained, a pardon may be issued.

As for general matters to be reported to the Emperor, after discussion and decision by the *Uin,* they are referred to the *Seiin* by the chief official in charge of them. Thereupon, the *Dajodaijin* reports to the throne; after imperial sanction is obtained, the matter will be referred back to that chief official for execution.

Documents and drafts of legislation and administration, imperial rescripts, records of appointments and dismissals, etc., are entrusted to the Secretariat. A special office *(Gaishi)* is responsible for customary announcements, ordinary instructions, etc.

Requests (legislation, etc.) by the chief official for imperial approval are classified by the Secretariat and prepared in duplicate. The original is countersigned by an *Uin* official and registered by the Secretariat; and

Appendix II

it is forwarded to the *Dajodaijin* who places his seal upon it. After it receives imperial approval, it is entrusted to the chief official for execution.

The business of the Secretariat, the various sections, and the Board of Ceremonies, in each case, is managed by a chief official.

3. *Sain.* The *Sain* discusses legislation. On matters concerning new administrative regulations, modifications of existing laws, and non-legal matters, the *Sain* holds detailed discussions. Thereafter, depending upon the will of its members, it drafts legislation and passes upon it. Thereupon, after signature, the bill, etc., is presented to the chairman and transmitted to the *Uin.* Although the *Sain* has the power to discuss legislation thoroughly, it does not have the power to make final decisions. However, unless legislation, etc., is discussed and approved by the *Sain*, even though it be decided by the *Uin*, transmitted to the *Dajodaijin*, and receive imperial approval, it may not be put into operation.

The *Sain* is composed of ordinary and extraordinary members. Ordinary members serve in this body regularly. Extraordinary members are selected from among Department administrators. On occasions when legislation is before the *Sain* that is pertinent to their Department, they attend and participate in the discussion.

A Legislative Section is attached to the *Sain.*

4. *Uin.* The *Uin* is made up of the Emperor, the *Dajodaijin*, the Councillors, and Ministers of the various Departments. It deliberates upon and approves legislation, etc.; and its decision is reported to the Emperor by the *Dajodaijin.* When the *Uin* discusses extremely important business, the Emperor is present if he is available. Unless legislation, decrees, etc., have the approval of the *Uin*, even though they are reported by the *Dajodaijin* and approved by the Emperor, they may not be enforced. On all business, all the members present confer and decide. When the members concur in their decision, without exception, all sign and bear responsibility equally although only one of them may be chiefly in charge of the matter.

The *Uin* has two or three secretaries who record in summary form the deliberations made known to them by those Councillors on duty on a given day. When both the *Udaijin* and *Sadaijin* are in attendance, the *Udaijin* usually presides. If those Councillors who are present have no additional office in Departments, they may possibly take care of the affairs of the *Uin.* In this case, there is no need for special duty officers.

* * * *

The three powers—legislative, administrative, and judicial—are distinct as functions of the state. Each has its own purpose. When these powers are not separated, the affairs of state are confused. There is not thorough debate or careful consideration of legislation. There is not sufficient time to establish good laws and make the execution of them effective; moreover,

Appendix II

it is impossible to decide whether legislation conforms to other laws. Everything is decided too hurriedly and carelessly; it is impossible to avoid numerous abuses. Moreover, when the three powers are entrusted to one body, it gives full rein to its power and follows its own self-interest. It legislates improperly and it is not restricted by a reasonable use of power. It arbitrarily enslaves the people, and it takes no notice of their difficulties. Without concern for the good of the nation, it arbitrarily gives way to its desires.

For this reason, in those European nations of long experience and proficiency in politics, the three powers are separated. The official sphere of each of the powers is delineated. The limits of the power of each are established by law. Each protects its own sphere and does not permit the slightest invasion of its prerogatives. When they established this kind of separation of power, they sought to base it on the original principle of government. I think that this is well suited to the political systems of their countries. In view of the condition of our country now and in the future, I do not think that we will be able to achieve a good government unless we turn our attention to the problem of the form of our government and establish a constitution at an early date. However, although we now try to model our government on the above style, separating the three divisions of power and seeking to prevent them from infringing upon each other, I cannot say profitably whether or not this has been achieved as expected. Hoping to achieve this aim and considering the future, I submit the following opinion.

1. Legislative

    An assembly is responsible for legislation. It is limited to the discussion of those matters cited in the general regulations. It may not enforce its decisions immediately. It discusses important matters according to rules of debate based upon the constitution. Its decisions are reported to the throne by the *Dajodaijin,* who seeks imperial approval.

2. Administrative

    The Departments and prefectures are responsible for this. They enforce matters reported to the throne by the *Dajodaijin* and approved by the Emperor. They enforce matters discussed and approved by the assembly according to the constitution.

3. Powers of the Emperor
    1. The Emperor possesses supreme power in the operation of the national administration.
    2. He hands down the throne.
    3. He appoints and dismisses officials of *chokunin* rank.
    4. He dispatches Ministers-Plenipotentiary.
    5. He sends special secret emissaries abroad.
    6. He convenes and dissolves the assembly.
    7. When discussions in the assembly are disadvantageous to the country, he terminates them.

APPENDIX II

8. He submits laws for discussion to the assembly.
9. He mobilizes and demobilizes the army.
10. He is not responsible for political mistakes.
11. He is not restricted by law.
12. He may, by a special order, have a justice question even one who is not defendant in a legal suit.
13. Except for the execution of rebels, after a court decision, he may mitigate capital punishment.
14. He grants rewards and declares punishments.
15. He grants or rescinds court rank.
16. He makes new nobles.
17. He grants or rescinds titles of nobility.
18. He commands the Army and Navy and administers all military and naval installations, including forts, warships, and arsenals. He also heads the reserve.
19. He establishes weights and measures.
20. He supervises the Imperial Family.
21. He may forbid the emigration of his subjects, and he may summon those who live abroad. He may banish his subjects from Japan.
22. He may treat foreigners the same as his people and may employ them.
23. He may grant licenses to foreigners.

4. The Assembly

It is composed of nobles *(kazoku)*, specially selected representatives, and Department Ministers. It discusses important affairs of state according to the constitution.

A chairman is elected by ballot from among the members. He manages the affairs of the Assembly.

The Assembly formulates its discussions according to the constitution and has its members maintain rules of debate. It must not concern itself with matters of administration.

5. General Principles for the Selection of Assemblymen

1. Persons more than twenty-one years of age who are heads of *kazoku* families elect representatives from among their number.
2. Twenty members represent the nobles *(kazoku)*. The others are selected by special order of the Emperor, and there is no limit on their number. The Emperor also has the power to make heads of Departments members.
3. A *kazoku* member may not be dismissed from office, even by the Emperor, unless he has committed a crime.
4. After two years, half of the *kazoku* members and half of the selected members are replaced. The remainder are changed after three years.
5. Except for the *kazoku*, the members receive an official salary.

Appendix II

6. Principles of Legislation
    1. The Assembly confers and agrees upon the amount of the budget. The estimates are studied by the Department of Finance and a draft is presented to the *Seiin* for discussion and approval. Thereupon, it is submitted to the Assembly.
    2. It discusses increases and changes in fixed taxes. In the case of unusual natural calamities, etc., when revenues are not sufficient, it confers and agrees upon ways to make up the deficit.
    3. It confers and agrees upon regulations imposing new taxes.
    4. It confers and agrees upon laws passed by the *Seiin*.
    5. It confers and agrees upon general regulations for business concerns.
    6. It confers and agrees upon methods and denominations of coinage.
    7. It confers and agrees upon methods to circulate and fund gold notes and establishes regulations concerning them.
    8. It confers and agrees upon means to levy and fund domestic and foreign debts.
    9. It discusses increases and decreases in the armed forces. However, in emergencies, this is the power of the Emperor.
    10. The decisions of the Assembly may not become law without imperial approval.
    11. If a bill is reported to the throne by the *Daijin* and promulgated without referral to the Assembly, the Assembly may object.

Appendix III

Draft Constitution of the *Genroin* 1878

Part I

Chapter I: The Emperor

Article I. The Japanese Empire shall be governed by an Imperial line unbroken for ages.

Article II. The person of the Emperor is sacred and inviolable.

Article III. The Emperor has the power of administration.

Article IV. The Emperor appoints and dismisses government officials.

Article V. The Emperor approves and proclaims laws.

Article VI. The Emperor commands the Army and Navy and dispatches them on occasion. The promotion, demotion, and resignation of military officers is decided by the Emperor according to law.

Article VII. The Emperor declares war, makes peace, and concludes treaties of communication and trade. However, treaties which expend national assets or alter national boundaries are not effective unless approved by both Houses of Parliament.

Article VIII. The Emperor has the power to pardon or reduce criminal sentences.

Article IX. The Emperor orders the minting of money.

Article X. The Emperor summons both Houses of Parliament, extends their sessions, and orders their adjournment.

Article XI. The Emperor grants titles of nobility and decorations.

Chapter II: The Succession to the Imperial Throne

Article I. The descendants of the reigning Emperor shall succeed to the Throne as rightful heirs.

Article II. The order of succession shall be the Crown Prince and his male descendants. They shall succeed according to the correct order of seniority among the legitimate sons. When the Crown Prince has no male heir, the succession shall be transmitted to the younger brothers of the Crown Prince or to the male heirs of elder or younger brothers of the Crown Prince. When there is no legitimate male heir, the illegitimate sons shall succeed, with the younger giving precedence to the older.

Article III. When there is no one of the Imperial line to succeed to the Throne in accordance with the order prescribed in the previous article, succession to the Throne shall be according to the degree of proximity of kinship among the various Imperial Princes.

Article IV. On special occasions when there is need to change the order of succession to the Imperial Throne, the approval of both Houses of Parliament shall be obtained.

Appendix III

Article V. In performing the ceremony of accession to the Throne, the Emperor shall take an oath to adhere to the National Constitution before a meeting of both Houses.

Chapter III: Minority of the Emperor and Regency

Article I. The Emperor shall attain majority at full eighteen years of age.

Article II. While the Emperor is a minor, he who is closest in kinship among the various Imperial Princes and who is over full twenty years of age holds office as Regent.

Article III. When there is no Imperial Prince, the Empress Dowager takes office as Regent.

Article IV. The provisions concerning the Regent as set forth above shall be followed when it is impossible for the adult Emperor to administer his powers himself. In this case, if there is a Crown Prince of full eighteen years of age, he shall take office as Regent.

Article V. The Regent takes an oath before a meeting of both Houses to serve the minor Emperor loyally and faithfully and to adhere to the National Constitution.

Article VI. While a Regent holds office, not a single revision of the Constitution may be made.

Chapter IV: Expenditures of the Imperial Family

Article I. The revenue for the Emperor and the various Imperial Princes is prescribed by law.

Article II. The expenses for the construction and repair of the Imperial Palace and the Detached Palaces are provided by the National Treasury.

Article III. The Empress, when widowed, and the Crown Prince when he reaches full eighteen years of age, receive revenue from the National Treasury. When the Crown Prince marries, the amount of the revenue is doubled. The amount of revenue is prescribed by law.

Part II: The Empire

Article I. All lands of the Empire now within its boundaries constitute the Japanese Empire.

Artile II. The boundaries of the Empire *(fu, ken, do, gun, ku)* may not be changed except according to law.

Article III. Special laws are applied to the Government and affairs of dependencies.

Part III: Rights and Duties of the People

Article I. All the Japanese people have rights. Possession and loss of these rights is decided by law.

Appendix III

Article II. The people are legally equal.

Article III. All persons living within the Empire receive protection for their person and property. Special provisions for foreigners are an exception to this.

Article IV. The people equally enjoy civil and private rights with the exception of special provisions decided by law. They may be appointed to civil and military offices.

Article V. In order to provide for national expenditures, the people have the duty to pay applicable taxes.

Article VI. The people have the duty to serve in the armed forces. The method of selection and the length of service are decided by law.

Article VII. Personal freedom may not be violated. Persons may not be arrested and imprisoned except according to law.

Article VIII. Freedom of movement may not be restricted with the exception of military service.

Article IX. A person's house may not be violated. Houses may not be entered and searched unless according to law.

Article X. When it is necessary to suspend articles of the Constitution in whole or in part for the protection of national safety in an emergency, it shall be decided by law.

Article XI. Personal property is inviolable. No one may be deprived of property unless according to law.

Article XII. Mail is private. Letters may not be seized unless according to law.

Article XIII. People may publish their opinions and ideas without prior examination, but they are held responsible for observing the laws.

Article XIV. The people have freedom to worship in their own faith. However, worship which is harmful to the people and the Government is forbidden.

Article XV. The people have the right to assemble peacefully without weapons and to form companies. The utilization of these rights is decided by law.

Article XVI. The people have the right to petition. But in the case of joint petitions, each person must sign. Companies which are legally recognized are permitted to petition as one name. On such occasions, it must be concerning company affairs.

Article XVII. The people may not receive titles, honors, or pensions from foreign nations without Imperial approval.

Part IV
Chapter I: Legislative Power

Article I. Legislative power is divided between the Emperor and Parliament. The Emperor submits bills to Parliament, and Parliament reports them to the Throne.

Appendix III

Article II. Parliament is made up of the *Genroin* (Senate) and the House of Representatives.

Article III. It is within the jurisdiction of legislative power to interpret dubious provisions of laws in order to provide the people with precedents.

Chapter II: The *Genroin* and Its Powers

Article I. *Genroin* membership is no more than thirty. The Emperor selects them from the following categories:
1. Imperial Princes
2. Princes
3. Nobles (*kazoku*)
4. Persons of *chokunin* rank
5. Persons who have been of service to the nation
6. Persons with a profound knowledge of politics and law

Article II. The Crown Prince is a Member of the *Genroin* and occupies the highest position. When he is eighteen years old, he may enter the *Genroin;* and when he is twenty years old, he has the power to express his own views.

Article III. The chairman and vice-chairman of the *Genroin* is selected by the Emperor from among the Members.

Article IV. Besides its legislative power, the *Genroin* does the following:
1. It prosecutes crimes of the *Daijin* (*Daijin,* Councillors, Ministers of Departments, and top officials).
2. It approves treaties with foreign powers and changes in the order of succession. At the accession of an Emperor or the beginning of a Regency, it hears the oath.
3. It reports written opinions concerning bills to the Emperor.
4. It receives written opinions concerning bills.

Article V. The *Genroin* may request the presence of a *Daijin* and have him give his opinion in person. However, the *Daijin* has no vote.

Article VI. A Member may not be dismissed in spite of court action unless by his own request or because of old-age retirement.

Article VII. A Member receives an annual stipend of not more than six thousand yen or less than three thousand yen.

Chapter III: The House of Representatives and Its Rights

Article I. The House of Representatives is composed of Members elected according to regulations determined by law. There is at least one Member for each 150,000 people.

Article II. Representatives are elected by ballot and may be re-elected.

Article III. Persons eligible to be Representatives must be Japanese of twenty-five years of age who pay taxes to be determined by the election regulations. It is important that they fulfill the necessary conditions.

Appendix III

Article IV. The term of office of Representatives is four years. Every two years, half of the total number is re-elected.

Article V. During the session of the House of Representatives, five names are placed in nomination by the Members for the offices of Chairman and Vice-Chairman. They are reported to the Emperor for his selection.

Article VI. Representatives receive traveling expenses and *per diem* allowances according to law.

Chapter IV: General Rules for the Two Houses

Article I. Unless more than half of the Members of each House is present, a meeting may not be opened.

Article II. Each House decides matters by majority vote.

Article III. The sessions of each House are public. However, by the request of the Chairman or of more than five Members secret sessions may be held.

Article IV. Members may not be removed from office for opinions expressed in connection with their duties. Conformance with the regulations of each House is an exception to this.

Article V. Members, except in the case of flagrant offenses, may not be arrested and detained without the consent of their chamber.

Article VI. No one may serve as a Member of both Houses at the same time.

Article VII. In obtaining approval of bills, if both Houses cannot be opened at the same time, one of them may approve the legislation. This is reported to the other House when it opens.

Article VIII. Members take an oath to uphold the Constitution.

Part V: Administrative Power

Article I. The Emperor appoints and dismisses the *Daijin*.

Article II. Laws and documents which fall under their responsibility are countersigned by one of the *Daijin*.

Article III. The *Daijin* take an oath to uphold the Constitution.

Part VI: Judicial Power

Article I. Judicial power is administered in High and Low Courts in the name of the Emperor. The Courts adhere to no power but law.

Article II. Persons who have served for three years as judges appointed by the Emperor may not be removed even by Court order unless on their own request or because of retirement for old age.

Article III. The organization and powers of the Courts are decided by law. Special Courts may not be established unless they are based on the provisions of law.

Appendix III

Article IV. Army and Navy Courts use special laws.

Article V. There is one Supreme Court *(Daishinin)*.

Artile VI. The Supreme Court, besides its official duties according to law, judges charges against the *Daijin* that are prosecuted by the *Genroin*.

Article VII. Public prosecutors of the Supreme Court and the Courts are appointed and dismissed by the Emperor.

Article VIII. Civil and criminal cases are tried publicly. However, matters prejudicial to national safety and public morals may be tried in closed session.

Article IX. Reasons must be given for decisions of the Courts.

Article X. Judges and prosecutors take an oath to uphold the Constitution.

Part VII: Prefectural, Town, and Village Assemblies

Article I. There is an assembly in each prefecture and *fu;* and there is an assembly in each town and village. The method of selecting their members is decided by law.

Article II. The powers and duties of these assemblies are decided by law.

Part VIII: Finance

Article I. Each year the administration sends to the House of Representatives a Budget estimate for the coming year and a report on projected expenditures; and it transmits to the House a report on the collection of taxes and expenditures. The government must submit these to the examination of the House and obtain its approval.

Article II. Taxes may not be levied unless established by law.

Article III. There are no exemptions in the payment of taxes.

Article IV. The national debt may not be increased unless approved by law.

Article V. The quantity, material, and denomination of coins and the circulation of paper money are decided by law.

Part IX: Amendment of the Constitution

Article I. The legislative power includes the power to decide that it is necessary to modify an article of the Constitution.

Article II. Amendment of the Constitution requires that at least two-thirds of the Members of both Houses be present and that two-thirds of this quorum approve.

Supplementary

Article I. From the day that the Constitution goes into effect laws in conflict with it are abolished.

Article II. The oaths to uphold the Constitution taken by the Emperor and the various officials must be taken immediately after the Constitution goes into effect.

Appendix IV

Yamagata Aritomo's Opinion on Constitutional Government 1879

This memorial is presented to the throne by your servant, Aritomo. It is now twelve years since the Restoration was achieved under the grace of the throne, and during this period many reforms and social changes have occurred. The extension of imperial rule compares with the glorious era of Engi [901-914] long ago, and the august virtues of the Emperor compare with the benevolent rule of the Emperor Nintoku.

From a political standpoint, everything that has been accomplished was an absolute necessity of the times. We have established modern transportation such as trains and ships, a mail system, the telegraph, and universities and lower schools; and we have revised the land-tax, conscription, and the penal code. We have inaugurated plans for the encouragement of industry, commerce, and agriculture, a fixed monetary system, and standard weights and measures. Business associations are flourishing. This is all part of our program to strengthen agriculture, encourage business and commerce, and enrich the nation. In addition, everything was done to expand the army and navy in order to keep peace at home and to defend the nation from foreign countries.

The countries of the West are proud of their civilization, but what we have achieved does not differ greatly in principle. However, because the period since the Restoration has been so brief, we have not yet reached maturity. Such is what the government has established and implemented. However, considering the state of popular sentiments, we have to wonder why we see things go contrary to the results which we might expect.

When we consider the tendencies of popular sentiments today, the people have no respect for the government nor do they submit to its laws. They are apt to be suspicious. Why have the people reacted in this way to the program, outlined above, that the government has carried out? This program sought to enrich the people and to ensure their well-being. There was no self-interest upon the part of the government nor was there anything harmful to the people. However, the people are not appreciative; on the contrary, they seem to be rebellious and grow more and more suspicious.

If we cannot understand this by ordinary reason, we must now study its causes more profoundly. First, although the Restoration was a great achievement, it was not accomplished gradually. There is not always enough time to make the necessary adjustments to such a sudden change. Secondly, although the Restoration rid the traditional administration of abuses and established better policies, generally these have been surface changes. We cannot yet see the results of those sudden changes which are in the realm of reform. Thirdly, during the twelve years since the Restoration, old practices were generally abolished and systems based on new laws were established. As a result of these changes, there are some who have gained

Appendix IV

much happiness, but also, there are many others who lost their property, wealth, and position, principally the old military class (samurai) as well as a numerous army of formerly wealthy landowners and merchants who now suffer economic distress. Lastly, since the Restoration, we have modeled our legislative system on the West, and the people have come to know that we should maintain society by laws. However, we failed to realize that we must also govern society with good morals and customs. By this failure, we instigated numerous evils. Under the influence of these, young men and students are apt to scorn their fathers and brothers at home and, outside, hold their elders in contempt and think of their teachers as their servants.

Still more, as manners and customs deteriorate, people struggle for wealth and position in society and argue about trivial matters. As the theory of freedom was introduced into the country from abroad and gained popularity, the people erroneously thought that freedom meant to act arrogantly and as they pleased with no regard for others. There are some who take pride in denouncing government officials and in slighting superiors and elders, though they cannot control themselves and manage their own affairs. Love and respect of superiors and a feeling of kindness toward people are something of the past. Affectation for fashion and thoughtlessness are common now in society. How can we talk of morality and propriety? Although this condition is not attributable to government orders, it is still the result of evils arising from the tendency to maintain society solely by the power of laws. If we do not take note of this now before it is too late, the situation is bound to become critical. These four points are the causes of the general tendency for the people to lack respect for the government, to refuse to comply with its orders, and to entertain suspicions. Therefore, so far as we look at this on the surface, we may say that the laws of the government are not responsible for these results. However, if we look into the reality of the situation, should we ever say that they are not the cause?

On the other hand, there could be a question as to whether the points listed above were really inevitable. They have been inevitably produced out of the circumstances of the situation. That is to say, advantages are followed by disadvantages: when one thing occurs, it will be followed by another. Indeed, the successful achievement of the Restoration has led the nation on the road of peace, thanks to the immense imperial virtues, though not without difficulties arising along the way. Over the issue of the Korean expedition, the cabinet was divided [1872-73]; warfare broke out in Saga [1874]; there was the Yamaguchi Affair [1874]; and finally, there came the Satsuma Rebellion [1877]. Moreover, with the Formosan expedition [1874] and the Korean question [1876], fighting broke out four times and almost a fifth. In these times, the sentiments of the people did not lie with the central government, and it was difficult for the government to consider other matters or the future.

Appendix IV

Fortunately, with the greatness of the Emperor's morality and the firmness of the cabinet, we achieved a mighty accomplishment. However, can we say that we suppressed these outbreaks because our position was as firm as a rock? Indeed, the people now despise the government, do not comply with the laws, and entertain suspicions just as they did in the old days. A careful study of the present situation shows that at home the people are alienated from the government, and abroad there are problems in our relations with neighboring countries and the need for treaty revision.

Because of this, now is the time for us to make the foundation of the government solid. As for the method to accomplish this, it is our urgent task to effect a broadening and adjustment of power by a separation of the three powers—administrative, legislative, and judicial. If this is not done and suddenly there is an emergency, once again we will have to worry. It goes without saying that in such a situation, the prestige of the throne will gradually decline and respect for the Emperor will diminish. Not only will the government become an object of hatred, but I am afraid I must say something which any imperial subject should not mention. This bothers me greatly. Perhaps I am being unduly concerned, but I feel I must venture to speak my mind.

It is not unique for statesmen to direct popular sentiment to lie with the government. To attain that objective, they must appropriately put into practice the demands of the common people. That is, they must establish a constitution. This has been anticipated by the government. For example, a rescript was presented to the *Genroin* in September 1876 directing it to draft a constitution. This is something which will be established sooner or later, but it is not an easy task. As for a constitution, it will set up a basic law of the land. It will be handed down through the ages as the unshakable foundation of the nation which the sovereign must guard firmly together with the people. Of course, although it cannot be drafted in a day and a night, we can set up general rules. If we base the administration of cabinet affairs and the limitations of the powers of officials on them, then the direction of the government's plans will be settled, and we can expect that this will gain popular support. Although there is, of course, no argument on the point that the constitution should lay down that the land should be forever governed by an Emperor of an unbroken family lineage, landownership certificates have already been given to the people. And since the landholdings of the Emperor have been limited, the private property and wealth of the imperial family must be provided for separately. Moreover, an annual stipend for the Emperor must be established.

Still more, it is a matter of course that we should promulgate and conform, with the people, to a constitution which we may obtain by compiling those laws which have already been promulgated and enforced. We must not leave even a point of doubt about them so that their provisions may be harmonious and thoroughly consistent with the operation of the administra-

Appendix IV

tion, the powers of the assembly, and the decisions of courts. This will not necessarily be difficult.

Although we have already laid the basis for the separation of the three powers—administrative, legislative, and judicial—for the most part, there will not be contradictions in the constitution if we adhere strictly to this separation, establish the boundaries of the powers, and do not have the administration restrain the other two powers. Although this cannot be worked out well in a day and a night, if we follow such a plan sincerely and spend a number of years on it, gaining experience gradually, we will reach our proper goal.

What is most difficult is to define the powers of the Emperor and the rights of the people. The Emperor has handed down the Rescript of 1875, based upon the Charter Oath of 1868, and we are striving to attain gradually a constitutional form of government. About that time [1875], we convened the *Chihokankaigi* (Assembly of Prefectural Governors), and this year we are convening prefectural assemblies. With these as a starting point, we have adopted an orderly method to reach our goal.

Now that we have come this far, we may perhaps advance to the point of establishing a popular assembly. However, this body is the place where the powers of the Emperor and the people are divided. Its importance is much greater than the prefectural assemblies and its purpose is different. If a popular assembly is established, the basic element of the nation's constitutional system will be formed. Then, it will not be difficult to build up the other branches of government. If the assembly has extensive power, we must be careful not to establish it too quickly. However, we need not be wise men to know that it will have to be done sooner or later. It is an important measure and an inevitable development, and we should be aware that it bears upon control of the nation and, at worst, it might invite a grave disaster for the country. Thus, we should actually establish it without making any prior declaration. If we establish an assembly with a minimum of fanfare, we can experiment with it. Then, when there is no discontent, it will not be too late to change its name and make a public announcement. If we decide to convoke an appointed body, it will be a matter of political strategy. If the members are specially selected, we can choose able and intelligent men. Fortunately, we have already established the prefectural assemblies, and it is easy to distinguish the leading figures in them. We should convene the assembly by selecting their ablest members. First have the members discuss the provisions of the constitution; then have them proceed to a discussion of the various provisions of legislation for the country. After some years of experience, if this body proves deserving of legislative power, then it should be transformed into a popular assembly. Or perhaps, we should not adopt an appointed house but have two or three members elected by ballot from each prefectural assembly. Thus after we have had experience, we may combine the systems of indirect election and

Appendix IV

transform the chamber into a popular assembly. Such a body should, of course, not be given the name popular at the outset. The power of convening and dissolving this body shall rest with the government in the beginning, and we should also decide that its decisions may not always be implemented.

Some people may question whether this is not a second *Genroin* and a foolish doubling of the expenses of official salaries. There is some reason in this criticism. However, the *Genroin* is a place which has men of ability such as members of the imperial family and officials over the 4th or 5th grade. The assembly will be made up of men of ability over twenty-five years of age from the prefectural assemblies. The bodies are not at all the same. Would not the imperial court sincerely pursue a course whereby this appointed assembly will be transformed into a popular assembly in the future? Others will say, if its powers are too limited, the assembly will simply follow the will of government officials; and thus, it will not be worth while. But this is not true either. Although the people of the nations of western Europe have the right to participate in the national administration, comparing our nation to these countries, we cannot expect to attain their level. However, we are just making a start. How can people judge that our policy is useless? There will be others who will say that this stems from intrigue and is not just. However, we will act in good faith and with political foresight. Generally, in administering affairs of state, how can there be anyone who does not consider the advantages and disadvantages in adherence to justice. It will be our principle to make this assembly the foundation on which to erect a firm popular body in the future, but I should not go into detail about this here. However, according to this plan, if we gradually establish a popular assembly and firmly establish a constitution, the things that I enumerated above—popular enmity towards the government, failure to follow government orders, and suspicion of the government, these three evils—will be cured in the future. There will be no need to worry about popular sentiment even if there might be agitation.

Although my anxiety is perhaps too great, I speak of these things for your majesty's sake. The reason I spoke in detail was that I hope that we can develop an opportune program through political strategy and manage the affairs of state properly. However, since this is not something that can be understood in a moment, we must take sufficient time for it. In brief, although there is a preferred order in dealing with such a matter, I hope that we can carry out the will of the imperial rescript [of 1875], win over public sentiment, and carry out policies orderly. Moreover, if there is a better way and if the people will be satisfied with it, I will not raise any objection to it. My motives in writing to your majesty are nothing but those ideas referred to in this memorial.

Appendix V

Ito Hirobumi's Opinion on Constitutional Government 1880

I, Hirobumi, am most concerned and fearful to take this opportunity to express my views. Occupying an important post in government, I feel deeply that the times are critical. I, for one, am convinced that now is the time to make unprecedented reforms and that conditions are already ripe for them. However, we must not follow the increasing thoughtless opinions; at the same time, it will be difficult to maintain old practices unconditionally. In politics, it is best to adopt methods that fit changing circumstances. Unless we take suitable measures and advance properly as well as gradually, how can we hope to lay the foundations of lasting peace?

We know now that the work of the Restoration has been nearly accomplished; yet the current situation may well suddenly become a crisis. There are two reasons why we cannot safely be at ease. I will first discuss these reasons and then suggest suitable measures to adopt.

1. The government of the Restoration revised the old and established the new. One of these great changes was *haihan chiken* (abolition of the *han* and issuance of land certificates). The implementation of *haihan chiken* was inevitable. At the same time, the conscription system was established. As a result, the number of those samurai who were deprived of their stipends and lost their property amounted to several hundred thousand throughout the country. None of them was happy with the Restoration government and all of them longed for the old practices. They voiced their discontent and complained bitterly. In extreme cases, they were moved to rebel and resist the government, thus intensifying political crises. This is one of the causes of the current difficulties.

The samurai had ranked higher than commoners in feudal days. Previously, they received regular stipends, had property, and were well educated. They used to take upon themselves the responsibility for state affairs; and thus today, they take pleasure in political debates. It is from among the former samurai that most of the men of spirit and argument have come. The commoners readily follow the ex-samurai. To take the human body as an analogy, the ex-samurai are the muscles and bones and the commoners are the flesh and skin. When the muscles and bones move, the flesh and skin follow. When the ex-samurai organize the various sources of discontent, they alienate the people from the government and stand in the way of the benevolent influence of the Emperor. Today, the attitude of the ex-samurai is not good for the imperial family, and a source of trouble for the whole nation is often concealed in it.

2. It is easy to control the popular sentiments of a single village, but it is difficult to control the public opinion of an entire nation. Moreover, it is easy to change the conditions of a country, but it is difficult to alter world-

Appendix V

wide trends. Today, conditions in Japan are closely related to the world situation. They are not merely the affairs of a nation or province. The European concepts of revolution, which were carried out for the first time in France about one hundred years ago, have gradually spread to the various nations. By combining and complementing each other, they have become a general trend. Sooner or later, every nation will undergo changes as a result.

In this period of changes from old to new, revolution often broke out. In fact, revolution continues at present. It has not yet stopped. Elsewhere enlightened rulers, with the help of wise ministers, led and controlled these changes, thus solidifying their nations. In brief, all have had to discard absolutist ways and share political power with the people.

Now, European ideas and things are coming into our country like a tidal flow; moreover, new opinions concerning the form of government have become popular among the ex-samuai. Within a few years' time, these ideas have spread into the towns and countryside, and this trend cannot be halted immediately. Thus, there are persons who surprise the public by voicing misleading views. Their thoughtless, disorderly acts pay no attention to the considerations of the Emperor. They groan although they are not sick, and their violent acts have evil effects upon others. However, if we take a general view of causes, it appears that this experience is common to the whole world. Like the rain falling and the grass growing, it is no wonder that we, too, have been affected.

These above two factors are what the trends of the time have brought about, and human efforts cannot control them. At present, it is the responsibility of the government to follow a conciliatory policy and accommodate itself to these tendencies so that we may control but not intensify the situation, and relax our hold over government but not yield it. We must follow the path of orderly progress and take our time in order to reach proper standards. Should we not consider the following plan carefully?

1. I ask that we enlarge the *Genroin* and select its members from among the nobles *(kazoku)*.

I say that we should not establish a parliament hastily. This does not mean that we, the ruling group, want to remain at the helm of state and occupy the highest posts as long as possible. Although it is very desirable to establish limited monarchy by convoking a parliament, we must not do anything that would seriously modify our national polity [the Emperor system]. We should first make the footings firm, then erect the foundation posts, and finally raise the house. This must be done in an orderly fashion. Needless to say, the above is clearly known to the intelligent mind of the Emperor.

When I consider the constitutional nations of Europe, the upper and lower houses, like the two wheels of a cart, complement each other and are in balance. In the monarchial nations, the *Genroin* or upper house is

Appendix V

essential to maintain the nation. In the various nations of Europe, the members of the upper house are selected from mature statesmen, men of merit, and erudite scholars. Moreover, in monarchial nations, they are selected largely from the nobility and they protect the royal family and maintain old practices.

I think that if we now wish to carry out change according to some gradual program and wish to enact reforms progressively, we first should enlarge the *Genroin* and have it actually conform to its name. If we wish to make the *Genroin* conform to its name, we should select its members from the nobles and ex-samurai *(shizoku)*. The *Genroin* was established in 1875, actually the result of the Emperor's intention to advance gradually towards constitutional government. When Kido and Okubo agreed to it, their objective was principally to protect the government and the people. But at that time, only its form was decided. There was not time to develop its practical uses. Now is the time to enlarge it and extend its functions, and make it live up to its name. At present, viewing the quality of our people, we find that the ex-samurai are the only ones who can manage national affairs and who are the most enlightened. Thus, the ex-samurai must be considered as one part of the nobility, though actually they rank just below the nobles. The members of the *Genroin* should be selected from among the nobles and ex-samurai as well as from among those persons who are eminent for their services to the country or for their scholarship. There should be one hundred members of the *Genroin* and each member should be paid. We should convene the *Genroin* each year for a definite length of time. If the drafts of all laws are submitted for discussion to the *Genroin*, the following results will be obtained:

1. We can employ ex-samurai in posts of honor, thereby enabling them to function through many ages as guardians of the imperial family.
2. We can provide a ground on which equilibrium will be maintained between the two houses of parliament in the future.
3. Through the *Genroin,* we can establish and maintain harmony between the government and the people.
4. Thus, we can continue the fine results of the past eight years, and following the plans of our forerunners, we will tread the path of gradual progress.
2. I ask that we establish an extra Board of Auditors.

I think that in addition to broadening public opininon by selecting *Genroin* members from among the nobles and ex-samurai, we should select members of the prefectural assemblies to fill positions as extra auditor-representatives who will discuss finance publicly. This will be the initial step towards constitutional government. It is observed in every country that some people despise their government and its officials because they suspect that a great deal of money raised by heavy taxation is spent wastefully. So

Appendix V

it is considered to be most important in all constitutional states to permit the people to participate in the management of national finance.

Since the Restoration, our country has spent a vast amount of money not only because of the expenses incurred from the many years of abuses under the Tokugawa regime, but because of successive wars, disturbances, and frequent diplomatic emergencies. However, we have raised an army and navy, reformed the law codes, extended education, made the police more efficient, constructed prisons, begun railroads and the telegraph, and opened new roads—all advantages for the people. We have used the whole strength of the nation on things for public benefit and utility. On the other hand, we have revised the land tax and enriched the farmers and encouraged various industries through loans. Everything that we have done has been at the expense of the upper classes and for the benefit of the lower classes. That is why the national treasury has been nearly exhausted during these ten years.

However, the government's finances have always been managed honestly. Nothing suspicious or dishonest was done. When later ages examine our record, there will not be the slightest mistake of which we should be ashamed. People who do not know the facts make accusations against the authorities, and what is worse make up rumors to slander them. In the government, there is little knowledge of this talk. But the government can show the public what it has done and make the people understand how correctly it has managed the national finances.

At present, an extra Board of Auditors should be established with its members selected from among the members of the prefectural assemblies. They should be compensated according to their work. Together with the regular auditors, they should engage in the business of auditing finances. However, their powers should be limited only to auditing, and they should not be permitted to interfere in general financial policies. By this method, for one thing, we can pave the way for public discussion of finance and, second, we can acquaint the people with the actual state of affairs and give them experience.

If these two proposals are carried out, we may expect that there will inevitably be some limitations on the administrative power compared with previous days. However, this will be an important responsibility for your ministers. When we develop methods of government improperly, public agitation will increase and friction will be intensified. We do not know if our mistakes will cause any disturbances. We must exercise the greatest caution. The organization, limits of power, and the method of selecting the members of these bodies are the keys to tranquillity. The ministers of state must not treat these matters lightly. The authority of deciding and carrying out these plans belongs only to the Emperor.

3. I ask that Your Imperial Majesty declare the aims of the nation.

Appendix V

If we do not decide the aims of the nation, what will stop popular sentiments from drifting? At present, there are persons who are stirring up the disorderly elements in town and country in the name of public opinion. If we fail to check such public sentiment by clearly revealing the will of the Emperor, based on some firm proposal, the people will unite to make disturbances, rising here and there like rivers overflowing their banks. Once violence bursts out like this, I fear that in the end an adjustment cannot be made. The orders of previous governments proclaimed only fundamental principles and did not give details. The uninformed would say that they did not carry out what they promised. Resentful persons would distort the Charter Oath and the Imperial Rescript of 1875 in support of their views. This is why the government should inform the people of its intentions and make them aware of actual conditions. If we wish to promote the government plans of the past eight years and check headstrong public sentiment, I suggest the following:

Your Majesty should kindly make up his mind and show his utmost sincerity by an imperial edict. I beg that you inform the people that the nation should advance gradually, and make your plans clear to them. How to share the legislative power with the people is without doubt a matter that comes under the supreme power of the Emperor and which is beyond the right of discussion by his humble subjects. Moreover, the timing of the decision is left to the discretion of the Emperor, and the people are not permitted to make disturbances or put on pressure.

The Emperor has issued a rescript gradually instituting constitutional government. It will reach fulfillment in a matter of years. In the meantime, the Emperor will be in control of the matter, and I think that he holds himself most responsible. If an imperial rescript is issued explaining that this policy is just, those persons who are loyal to the imperial family will be reminded of the direction in which they should turn their sentiments. On the other hand, unenlightened people will avoid being led astray to acts of violence. These are the most ardent desires of this humble servant of Your Majesty.

I wish also to say that although Your Majesty's august virtues date back to the remote ages, still these times are hard beyond comparison with previous reigns. From now on, we will depend solely upon Your Majesty's courage and vigor to encourage truth, superintend overall policies, maintain definite principles, turn what is a crisis into a peaceful situation, and finally to perfect the government as a whole through gradual progress. This will depend upon the courage of Your Majesty. This is not a mere matter of words. I, Hirobumi, beg to remain, Your Majesty, your most respectful and fearful servant.

Appendix VI

Okuma Shigenobu's Opinion on Constitutional Government 1881

1. The date for the establishment of a parliament should be promulgated.

When the people's minds advance greatly but the laws of the land lag far behind, this divergence causes the downfall of the laws. And when the minds of the people are backward and the laws are more advanced, the laws do not benefit the country. When advanced persons are not too numerous and those who are backward are fewer, it is better to improve the laws and thereby make them conform to the public mind.

Since last year, there have been many persons who have petitioned for the establishment of a parliament. Although there are various criticisms of their character and conduct, all things considered, the persons responsible for these petitions are symptomatic of a public spirit seeking to advance gradually. When I consider the public sentiments, I find very few backward people. Thus, it may be safe to say that the time has come to reform the laws and to establish a parliament.

When the people's minds advance gradually and the laws remain more or less backward, the drift of public sentiment is directed exclusively to the reform of the laws. Thus, ideas which are essential to the people in seeking to stand firm in the face of foreign nations and ideas which seek to improve the nation in other ways will be discarded by the people, who will have only an intense desire to reform the laws. This is a disadvantage for the country.

In consideration of the degree of intelligence of our people and the desire for national stability, we should carry out the Imperial Rescript of 1875, which sought to establish constitutional government gradually through reform of the laws. This is the general principle I put forward today. This is the foundation on which to build. I ask that we quickly promulgate the date for the establishment of a parliament, set up a committee to draft a constitution, and begin the construction of a parliament building. (The date for the establishment of a parliament is discussed in detail in section 5.)

2. High officials should be appointed on the basis of the support of the people.

When the Emperor selects and appoints officials, he should consider the confidence of the people. However, in an absolutist form of government, there is no place for an indication of popular confidence. Thus, it is inevitable that, considering achievements and services, he select intelligent persons in whom he would judge the people put their confidence, and make them his advisers. In systems of government where there is a place for an indication of popular confidence, it is a matter of course to appoint officials in consideration of the people's will. When officials are appointed in this manner, the right persons will be called in, and the Emperor will be even more esteemed.

Appendix VI

In constitutional government, the place where the will of the people can be indicated is indeed the parliament. What do I mean by "will of the people?" It is the will of more than half of the parliamentary representatives. Who commands this will? It is the leader of the political party that has a majority in parliament. Because parliament is the place where the representatives indicate the opinions of the people who elected them, the will of the representatives is the will of the people. When we consider a political party that has won the support of the majority of the people, is it not the person who is esteemed as its leader who reflects their will?

A constitutional form of government produces an excellent arena where the Emperor can easily recognize such a man. Not only does he avoid actually making the selection himself, but he keeps the nation blessed with tranquillity. Because a person who is appointed in this way has a majority in parliament where the people participate in government, he has the power to control the legislature. And because he has his position in the government with the favor of the Emperor and places the members of his party in important positions, he also has the power to control the administration. Thus, there is no clash between the legislature and the administration, and the overall operation of the government stems from one source. Only in this way will the business of the government be put in order for the first time.

Let us consider the history of those countries which lacked political tranquillity under a constitution and suffered from political instability which led from time to time to conditions of confusion and disturbance. The cause of this misfortune was based everywhere upon the development of friction between the head of the administration and the leader of the political party which reflected the will of the people in the legislature because of the unwillingness of an administration to give up office or of the monarch to dismiss a favorite official. In the case of the famous constitutional nation, England, prior to 1782 this condition prevailed. However, after many years of continuous experience, from that year on, the monarch came to appoint the Prime Minister in consideration of his popularity, and he entrusted this responsible post to men who headed the majority party in parliament. Since that time, there has been no evidence of friction between the government and parliament. Party struggles were in parliament and did not extend to the government.

The secret of constitutional government lies in its essence, not in its forms. The separation of the three powers—legislative, administrative, and judicial—and the grant of popular participation in government are its forms. Its essence lies in appointing to the highest offices the leaders of the majority party in parliament and the unity of the government as a result. If the forms are adopted but not the essence, constitutional government paves the way for confusion in the national administration. If we argue from the standpoint of the responsibility of entrusting offices to the talented

Appendix VI

and from the standpoint of stable and tranquil government and if we observe examples of political confusion in nations, as I have already stated, the Emperor must appoint as high officials the persons who are leaders of the political party with the largest number of representatives in parliament. However, it may happen that the party which has the confidence of the people will lose its support according to its skill in administration, and majority power in parliament will be transferred to another party. In such a case, the Emperor will have to consider the will of the people and appoint to the paramount positions persons from the party that has obtained new strength.

It is vitally important that the change in high officials which is produced by shifts of party power in parliament be carried out in an orderly manner. Some sort of procedure like the one that follows is necessary for the change from old to new officials. When a cabinet is to be newly formed, with the Emperor's approval, the leader of the party which is judged to have a majority in parliament will be summoned and invited to form the cabinet. In this case, the leader who receives the imperial mandate will establish an administration by placing the persons who are party leaders in high posts. After that, publicly announcing their obedience to the imperial order, they enter the cabinet. The commission to form a cabinet is usually the prerogative of the leader of the party, but at times someone else in the party may be ordered to do so. However, though this be the case, the actual head of the administration will be the leader of the party. (In England there are occasional examples of this.) And when the Emperor is to discern the strongest party, it is advisable for him to ask for advice from members of the imperial family or from the three *Daijin*.

When the party which has organized the cabinet at last loses power in parliament, important bills submitted by the government will be attacked and often voted down in parliament. This is a sign that the cabinet and the party have lost power. In such a case, because there is no unity in the administration of the government, the declining party must resign from office as a rule. When it is clear that a party has lost power and when it clings to the government and does not resign the administration, the opposition party which has won power will make a motion that parliament declare whether or not the officials of the cabinet and administration have lost the confidence of parliament. In keeping with this motion, when it is decided by vote that there is a lack of confidence, parliament will report this to the Emperor and petition that since the cabinet lacks the confidence of parliament, the Emperor should select a new Prime Minister. If the declining political party still refuses to resign in compliance with the demand of parliament, the Emperor will dismiss it from office. (This is based on the example of England, etc. When the signs of a loss of power are apparent, it is customary to resign.) However, when the party in control of the government sees signs of a loss of power in parliament and is to face a vote of non-confidence, if it feels that a majority of the people support it and feels that the members of parliament are incorrectly in office, it should, with the approval of the Emperor, immediately dissolve parliament with the aim of achieving a majority for its party among the newly elected representatives. If it wins a majority, the cabinet continues. If it does not, the cabinet must resign. This power of dissolving parliament must be regarded as a last resort. (This power must be used with great care. If it is used too often, it may do great harm. In the case of England, it has been used only two or three times.) The above method of parties changing office is based in great part on the example of England.

3. The distinction between political party officials and permanent officials.

As I have said above, a rise and fall of parties causes a change of officials. An important question is—Should this change extend to all officials or just part of them? Generally all office work requires great proficiency. In short, in the case of government offices, there are numerous petty matters, and old laws and precedents are constantly consulted. If we wish to complete the greatest amount of business without delay at the smallest expense, it is very important to have a permanent staff of lower officials in the bureaus of the government. However, if these officials are subject to change with the parties, this will certainly be disadvantageous and inconvenient. If the position of these officials is related to the rise and fall of parties, it would be extremely inconvenient and intensify friction between the parties, developing feuds to the point of violence. Because of this, we should distinguish between those who issue orders and those who obey orders. The former as party officials should resign with the party; the latter as permanent officials (non-party officials) should have positions of life tenure. Among high-ranking officials who hold important offices, there are some that, for the sake of maintaining order and tranquillity, must not have connections with political parties. These will be neutral, permanent positions, a kind of life office. (This is based on the example of England.)

To briefly list the various party officials, they are Councillors *(Sangi)*, ministers, vice-ministers, bureau chiefs, the imperial tutor, and the Grand Chamberlain. These party officials will be for the most part persons who hold seats in the upper or lower house. (In general, this is based on the example of England. Because it will be necessary to discuss in greater detail the distinction between political and non-political offices when we establish the constitution, I present merely an outline here. The same holds true for what follows.) As for the kinds of permanent officials, with the exception of heads of government offices, vice-ministers, and bureau chiefs, they will be officials below *sonin* rank and petty officials. These officials are persons who cannot be members of parliament. (Example—same as above.) As for the neutral, permanent officials, these are the three *Daijin* (I hope that they will have no relation to parties and will assist the Emperor, and that they serve as advisers at times when the Emperor gives an order to a

Appendix VI

political party to form a cabinet. Thus, they should be non-party officials in order that they can consider our national interests impartially), military officials, and police officials. Because they strive to maintain order and stability, these three kinds of officials are expected to possess the virtue of impartiality. If these offiicials are closely connected with political parties, they will use military and judicial power to overwhelm the other parties. They will destroy order in the country, lose their impartiality, and cause confusion in society. They must regard neutrality and impartiality as their great virtues. These officials cannot be parliamentary representatives. (Example—same as above.) If there are signs that permanent or non-political officials become connected with political parties, their superior may make them resign. There are numerous disadvantages in government service in being connected with a chief who is a political official. (Example—same as above.)

4. With imperial approval, we should establish a constitution.

When rules are established in advance and men adhere to them, matters are easily settled. When rules have not been determined and men gather together, matters are not settled easily. Now at this time we wish to bestow upon the land an unprecedented form of government. It is important that it maintain society in peace and order. If the bridle is cut and six horses escape, order cannot be restored easily. We therefore wish to see first a constitution established with imperial approval, and according to this, representatives summoned. With regard to the establishment of a constitution as described above, it is my hope that we create a committee in the cabinet and immediately set to work. The establishment of a constitution is a very important matter, and the organization of the upper house, the right to vote for representatives of the lower house, etc., will require elaborate preparation. Since these matters shall be presented on the day that the constitution is established, I will not talk about them in detail now. As I stated above, the secret of constitutional government lies in its essence. It is important to keept the constitution extremely brief, that it be only an outline. It is also necessary that the constitution have two characteristics: (1) that it be clear where power is vested; (2) that the rights of the people be clearly stated. Even though party government is implemented, there will be unspeakable abuses in the government unless there are constitutional provisions which establish popular rights. I hope that constitutional provisions which define popular rights in detail are included in the constitution.

5. We should elect representatives by the end of 1882 and convoke parliament at the beginning of 1883.

I have already explained that because the true form of constitutional government is party government, the two branches of government, legislative and administrative, are united, and the government has a single root. In the final analysis, constitutional government causes the people's will to be expressed peacefully, without disturbance to the social order. However,

Appendix VI

now when there are no political parties in the country, if a parliament is suddenly established, a number of political parties will be quickly formed, but their foundation will not be strong. Moreover, in general, the people will not know what parties advocate what principles. As a result, the power of parties will constantly vacillate. Thus, I fear that an unfortunate state of confusion and conflict will prevail in the government, and that the political means upon which society depends for the maintenance of order will cause society to suffer disturbance. I must warn you of this danger. At present, parties do not exist because there is no place for them. Once there is official notification that we will establish a constitutional government, the birth of political parties will follow quickly. If we permit an interval of a year or a year and a half, each party can make its views known generally. The people can judge the advantages and disadvantages of this one or that one, and each individual can choose his own party. Then, if we elect our representatives and convoke a parliament, order in society will be maintained easily, and we can obtain the true advantages of constitutional government. Thus, it is important that the announcement of the establishment of a parliament be made soon. The time of its convocation must not be announced too suddenly. In consideration of all these reasons, I hope that we will decide to draft a constitution this year and promulgate it either at the end of this year [1881] or the beginning of the next [1882]. Then I hope that we will summon representatives by the end of 1882 and convene parliament for the first time at the beginning of 1883. I think that this will not be a grave mistake.

6. We should decide principles of administration.

Although a political party springs from several sources, generally, it is formed by people with the same principles of administration in mind. And then the reasons for the rise and fall of a party lie in whether or not its principles of administration win the support of the people. Because of this, party struggles are struggles between principles of administration. Victory or defeat is a victory or defeat for principles of administration. As I stated above, when we establish a constitutional system of government and appoint the Prime Minister in consideration of the popular will, we must form parties. When we want to form parties, we must decide principles of administration which we especially advocate. Thus, if we want the present cabinet to form a party, the most important factor in its formation would be to determine its principles of administration. After the date for the establishment of parliament is announced publicly, I hope that our present cabinet will immediately decide its principles of administration. As for principles of administration, I have opinions of my own. I will discuss them in detail on some other occasion.

7. General remarks.

Constitutional government is party government, and the struggles between parties are the struggles of principles. When its principles are

Appendix VI

supported by more than half of the people, a party wins control of the government. When the opposite is true, it loses control. This is the operation of genuine constitutional government, wherein lie real advantages. But if there is only the form and not the spirit of constitutional government, not only is it a misfortune for the nation but it will be also a calamity for those who administer the government. They will bequeath to later generations the bad reputation for being greedy for power. Even if they act from pure and sincere motives, the people will suspect that they think of power and personal gain. When they do attempt to bestow constitutional government, should they oppose the general rules operating in constitutional countries, throw away the true advantages of a constitution, and display evidence of a love of power, how can they not be disliked by the people? Still more, this greed for power is the seed of a quick fall from power! Relinquishing power is always a difficult thing for anyone to accept. Persons who earnestly desire to help their country do not accept it easily. If the present administrators who have amassed extensive power in the government establish a true system of constitutional government and do not cling to power, this will be sufficient to show their virtue. Although this is not an action related to the praise and censure of society, they cannot but feel a great satisfaction in their hearts. People generally say that the peace or instability of a nation depends mostly upon political practices. Is it not then the urgent task of those in power to establish the precedent of peacefully changing the party in power without disturbing the social order, and thereby politically opening the way for the people to enjoy a blessed life?

The above, I respectfully propose.

Appendix VII

Iwakura Tomomi's Opinion on Constitutional Government 1881
To the *Dajodaijin* and the *Sadaijin*:

We have not yet made a beginning on the matter of a constitution which we discussed the other day. I am very sorry that, unfortunately, I have been on leave because of illness. However, I might offer the following three suggestions for your careful consideration.

1. With regard to the establishment of a constitution, since it will probably be difficult to settle on its articles, the Emperor should decide on some fixed plan—a general outline and various articles. This should be handed down in the form of an imperial note to the *Daijin* to provide standards for a draft constitution. This fixed plan will be the basic document of government, and it will be a mirror to settle disagreements for hundreds of years. I hope that you will properly advise the Emperor of this.

2. Concerning the procedure for drafting the constitution, I hope that one of the following three methods will be selected:
    a. We openly establish a Constitutional Investigation Commission.
    b. A secretariat for the drafting of the constitution be set up in the Imperial Court with one of the *Daijin* appointed its president. After a draft constitution is completed in secret, it will be submitted to the cabinet for discussion.
    c. The Emperor in secret order three or four *Daijin* and *Sangi* (Councillors) to draft the constitution. The completed draft will be submitted to the cabinet for discussion.

3. While the drafting of the constitution is a matter of national importance, it seems to be doubtful whether there can be a perfect draft unless the cabinet is in agreement. Thus, before you decide on the method of drafting the constitution, I hope you will collect the opinions of all the Councillors.

I hope that you will carefully consider what follows. Concerning the drafting of the constitution, I have appended separately "General Principles," which I hope you will present to his majesty for his information. [A summary translation of these principles is included in the narrative of this book.]

First Opinion:

It is essential to decide first the proper time for the inauguration of constitutional government and the opening of parliament. Moreover, we must decide on a system of constitutional government that is suitable to our national polity and customs. If we assume that the time to inaugurate constitutional government is at hand, then we have reached the point of inquiring about various systems. Although the purposes of constitutional governments in the various nations of Europe are generally the same, the methods and procedures of each more or less differ according to the level

Appendix VII

of civilization, national polity, and customs. When parliament is weak, it only participates in the discussion of laws. When it is strong, it actually makes the laws. The power of parliament varies from country to country; however, the most powerful is the English Parliament (this excludes republics). The English Parliament has not only legislative power but also administrative power. An English proverb says, "Parliament can do everything but change men into women and women into men."

Why does the English Parliament have administrative power, too? According to the customary law of England, the king does not hold the reins of government himself. He entrusts them to the Prime Minister, who depends upon a majority in parliament, and the cabinet is formed by the leader of the majority party. When the majority party in parliament changes, the Prime Minister is changed in rotation, just as a wheel moves and brings about a reaction in another wheel. The king is thus controlled by the majority in parliament and he is subject to control by a party. In form, he does nothing more than formally proclaim the policies decided by the majority party. He is like a flag fluttering, right and left, in the wind. In name, administrative power belongs to the king; in reality, the head of the administration is the leader of the majority party in parliament. Administrative power, actually, is in the hands of parties in parliament. Although, in name, sovereignty is shared by the king and parliament, in reality, sovereignty lies chiefly in parliament. The king has power in name only. In the language of England, "The king reigns over the people, but he does not administer the affairs of state himself." This condition is not different from our country, where from the early middle ages the actual power of government was in the hands of the military.

In contrast to this, in Prussia, the king not only reigns over his people but actually administers the affairs of state. Although the legislative power is shared with parliament, the administrative power is in the hands of the king and is not transferred to others. The king appoints his Prime Minister without concern for the numerical status of parties in parliament. In actual circumstances, although he generally selects someone whom parliament will support, the administrative power is never subject to the control of parties in parliament.

Although there is no unity of opinion among scholars of politics on the similarities and differences of the above two systems, it may be said that generally each differs according to its national polity and the feelings of the people. If England were modeled on the Prussian system, civil war could not help breaking out. Similarly, if Prussia copied England, its peace would be unavoidably disturbed.

If we establish constitutional government in our country and convoke a parliament, we will be instituting something new for Japan. Shall we copy the party government of England and make the administration of the government responsible to the majority in parliament? Or shall we advance

Appendix VII

gradually, grant only legislative power to parliament, and make the organization of the chief officers of the administration the prerogative of the ruler, thus copying Prussia? The decision of the government in this matter will establish a permanent foundation for the future. It will bestow advantages or disadvantages for a hundred years, and thus it is a very important matter.

By English customary law, the party system is based upon two parties. Thus, there is a minority and majority party. At present, parties have not yet been organized in Japan. If they were to be organized, they would be divided into a number of small parties. A large organization could not be established. Let us assume the present cabinet, having only minority support, was dismissed. The party replacing it would be required to have the support of the people and command a majority. However, various small parties would flourish, vie for power, and not be able to unite. They would form one great voice in attacking the government in power, but when they achieved their desire and sought to form a cabinet, they would split into factions and struggle for power among themselves. The arena of administrative power would be like a battlefield. A would tumble, and B would fall. There would be no stability. There would not be time to consider how to manage the affairs of state and national emergencies. In the end, we would have to resort to arms. This is one difference between Japan and England.

In England, with the exception of bureau and section chiefs and judicial officers who are permanent officials, the ministers, vice-ministers, the secretary-general, etc., all are party officials. Each time that the majority in parliament changes and the cabinet falls, it is customary for the important officials to resign. In our country, if we decided to change the cabinet and looked for persons to replace the *Sangi*, ministers, vice-ministers, and deputy directors, with the exception of two or three men in the country, who would have the support of the people? Would the young and able people rise to struggle for power? This is a second difference between Japan and England.

Since the Restoration, the benevolent influence of the Emperor has not yet everywhere penetrated into the sentiments of the people. There is enmity towards the government because of the abolition of the *han*. To change the government according to the majority voice of the people, suddenly modeling it on the methods of English party government, would be equal to establishing parliament today and changing the cabinet tomorrow. Members of parliament would say that to hasten the cabinet change would protect the tranquillity of the country. I cannot help but suspect that they are overcome by the good results obtained in England and that their opinions do not reflect the conditions of our country. Constitutional government is a new concept to Japan, and we have not yet had any actual experience with it. If we move too fast, we may later regret it. Once it is

Appendix VII

bestowed, it will be impossible to rescind it later. Rather, I believe we should advance gradually on the model of Prussia, thereby leaving room for future improvements.

Second Opinion:

If we wish to make the selection of cabinet ministers the prerogative of the Emperor and not be controlled by parliament, we should rely on the following three provisions:

a. There shall be a clear statement in the constitution that the Emperor has the responsibility to select the *Daijin* and officials of *chokunin* rank. He shall appoint and dismiss them. When there is such a provision, actually he will appoint persons to the post of *Daijin* who have popular support and dismiss those who lack it. Thus, because the power of appointment and dismissal belongs to the Emperor, the ministers depend upon the favor of the Emperor and the trust of the nation, and they are not controlled by the opinions of the people. They make up their minds and adopt a fixed course. Even though they obtain only a minority vote in parliament on two or three legislative matters, the cabinet as a whole remains intact and does not have to alter its policy. This is based on the Prussian Constitution.

b. The constitution shall provide for the responsibilities of ministers, and divide them into instances of collective responsibility and individual responsibility. The French Constitution of 1875 provides that ministers are collectively responsible for the overall administration of the government and individually responsible for their own office. If ministers are generally collectively responsible as in the example of England, whenever one minister makes a mistake and is censured by parliament, all the ministers have to resign from their posts. In this situation, the cabinet is easily attacked by parliament, and it becomes a battlefield of frequent changes. If, in theory, the mistake of a minister is the responsibility of all the ministers, the business of the administration should not be divided into separate jurisdictions and should be discussed by all the ministers. The responsibility of each will be lessened. In England, there is a system of collective responsibility, by which the cabinet ministers are regarded as a collective organ of a party and as one individual. To establish the organization of the administration by a division into ministries is not the same thing as uniting members of the legislature and forming them into a group.

c. Our constitution must copy one article of the Prussian Constitution. Article 109 of the Prussian Constitution says: "Taxes of the previous year shall remain in force." This means that if the government and parliament cannot agree on the annual budget, the budget of the previous year becomes effective. This provision is the most important element in the Prussian Constitution because it sustains administrative power. Unless this article is included, parliament may attack the cabinet and may only give minority support to its important bills. Moreover, if the cabinet relies on the protection of the Emperor and does not resign, parliament may reject tax bills to

Appendix VII

force the cabinet to adhere to its views. In this case, the national treasury will not be paid the necessary funds.

Because parliament has the power to reject taxes which are the life-blood of the nation, party cabinets are formed according to the will of parliament in England, Belgium, and Italy. By this concession, the support of parliament is secured.

If we wish to form a cabinet with no regard for parliament on the model of Prussia, we must rely on the tax provisions of that country. If this is not the case, even though there is a provision whereby the Emperor dismisses and appoints ministers, it will not be effective. I believe that the above three items are necessary to maintain the principle of gradual development and to protect the happiness of the nation forever.

Third Opinion:

Among the three suggestions that are included in part two, the third is taken from Prussia. The articles of the Prussian Constitution are not satisfactory to scholars of politics. In their opinion, the Prussian Constitution has not avoided a degree of absolutism. They say that the Prussian Parliament has no power of its own.

Article II of Chapter VII of the *Genroin* draft constitution [this is from the revised draft. It is the same in the original draft of 1878] states: "Taxes may not be levied unless established by law." This clearly entrusts the power to levy taxes to parliament. Under this article, should parliament disagree with a government-sponsored tax bill, the people would be freed from the obligation to pay taxes. As a result, the national treasury would have nothing to disburse. If the tax power rests entirely in parliament, it is like a tiger hiding itself in the shade of a mountain. Cabinets will rise and fall, and imperial orders will be controlled. What can prevent this from happening? The radical scholars will be sufficiently satisfied.

The first suggestion (that the Emperor appoint and dismiss ministers) and the second suggestion (that we seek to avoid collective responsibility) are opposed to the opinions of those persons who advocate the establishment of a constitution now. Article IX of the private draft constitution presented by the *Kojunsha* [Keio University graduates] states: "Cabinet Ministers shall be of one mind, carry out foreign and domestic affairs, and be collectively responsible." Article XII states: "The Prime Minister shall be selected by the Emperor according to the will of the people. The other Ministers shall be appointed on the recommendation of the Prime Minister." Article XIII states: "Cabinet Ministers shall be members of the *Genroin* or the House of Representatives." Article XVII states: "When the opinion of the Cabinet and the opinion of the Parliament do not agree, the Cabinet Ministers shall resign or by special power of the Emperor, they shall dissolve the Lower House."

The basic intent of these articles is to establish a "collectively responsible cabinet form of government." Moreover, when the cabinet does not agree

Appendix VII

with parliament, it will thereupon resign from office and be replaced by one that has the support of parliament. This so-called concept of the alternation of party cabinets is something based on the model of England.

Thus, in my opinion, radical views are gradually spreading throughout the country at present, and the power of this tendency is increasing. When it goes to extremes, we seek to stop it. What worries me very much is that the authorities are concerned with theory and do not study differences between nations. Nor do they think of lasting results. If we wish to be content with novelties and make the formation of cabinets subject to the will of the people, it is analogous to sweat which, once having come out, does not go back to the body. Not only will this destroy our national polity, but it will not provide for the peace of the nation or the happiness of the people —with the exception of a few empty thoughts.

The establishment of constitutional government is indeed an extraordinary reform. Unless the government settles its policy, I do not know how all the discussions and disturbances will be stopped. Perhaps the people will not be satisfied with the principle of gradual progress. In carrying out my three suggestions, we must be aware of the possibility that public opinion will be stirred up and the clamor of argument will increase. The people, jostling against each other, will push forward with their demands. In order to establish something that is firm and permanent, I simply suggest that the decision of the Emperor and the plans of the *Daijin* should not be wrong. Thus, I have expressed my sincere views which I hope will be understood.

Appendix VIII

Imperial Rescript Promising the Establishment of a Parliament 1881

We, sitting on the Throne which has been occupied by Our dynasty for over 2500 years, and now exercising in Our name and right all authority and power transmitted to us by Our ancestors, have long had in view gradually to establish a constitutional form of government, and to the end that Our successors on the Throne may be provided with a rule for their guidance.

It was with this object in view that in the eighth year of Meiji [1875], We established the Senate, and in the eleventh year of Meiji [1878], authorized the formation of Local Assemblies, thus laying the foundation for the gradual reforms which We contemplated. These Our acts must convince you, Our subjects, of Our determination in this respect from the beginning.

Systems of government differ in different countries, but sudden and unusual changes cannot be made without great inconvenience.

Our ancestors in Heaven watch Our acts, and We recognize Our responsibility to them for the faithful discharge of Our high duties, in accordance with the principles, and the perpetual increase of the glory, they have bequeathed to Us.

We therefore hereby declare that We shall, in the twenty-third year of Meiji [1890], establish a Parliament, in order to carry into full effect the determination We have announced, and We charge Our faithful subjects bearing Our commissions to make, in the meantime, all necessary preparations to that end.

With regard to the limitations upon the Imperial prerogative, and the constitution of the Parliament, We shall decide hereafter and make proclamation in due time.

We perceive that the tendency of Our people is to advance too rapidly, and without that thought and consideration which alone can make progress enduring, and We warn Our subjects, high and low, to be mindful of Our will, and that those who may advocate sudden and violent changes, thus disturbing the peace of Our realm, will fall under Our displeasure.

We expressly proclaim this to Our subjects.

Appendix IX

Preamble to the Constitution of the Empire of Japan 1889

Having, by virtue of the glories of Our Ancestors, ascended the Throne of a lineal succession unbroken for ages eternal; desiring to promote the welfare of, and to give development to the moral and intellectual faculties of Our beloved subjects, the very same that have been favoured with the benevolent care and affectionate vigilance of Our Ancestors; and hoping to maintain the prosperity of the State, in concert with Our people and with their support, We hereby promulgate, in pursuance of Our Imperial Rescript of the 12th day of the 10th month of the 14th year of Meiji, a fundamental law of the State, to exhibit the principles, by which We are guided in Our conduct, and to point out to what Our descendants and Our subjects and their descendants are forever to conform.

The right of sovereignty of the State, We have inherited from Our Ancestors, and We shall bequeath them to Our descendants. Neither We nor they shall in the future fail to wield them, in accordance with the provisions of the present Constitution and of the law.

We now declare to respect and protect the security of the rights and of the property of Our people, and to secure to them the complete enjoyment of the same, within the extent of the provisions of the present Constitution and of the law.

The Imperial Diet shall first be convoked for the 23rd year of Meiji and the time of its opening shall be the date when the present Constitution comes into force.

When in the future it may become necessary to amend any of the provisions of the present Constitution, We or Our successors shall assume the initiative right, and submit a project for the same to the Imperial Diet. The Imperial Diet shall pass its vote upon it, according to the conditions imposed by the present Constitution, and in no otherwise shall Our descendants or Our subjects be permitted to attempt any alteration thereof.

Our Ministers of State, on Our behalf, shall be held responsible for the carrying out of the present Constitution, and Our present and future subjects shall forever assume the duty of allegiance to the present Constitution.

Appendix X

Constitution of the Empire of Japan 1889

Chapter I: The Emperor

Article I. The Empire of Japan shall be reigned over and governed by a line of Emperors unbroken for ages eternal.

Article II. The Imperial Throne shall be succeeded to by Imperial male descendants, according to the provisions of the Imperial House Law.

Article III. The Emperor is sacred and inviolable.

Article IV. The Emperor is the head of the Empire, combining in Himself the rights of sovereignty, and exercises them, according to the provisions of the present Constitutions.

Article V. The Emperor exercises the legislative power with the consent of the Imperial Diet.

Article VI. The Emperor gives sanction to laws and orders them to be promulgated and executed.

Article VII. The Emperor convokes the Imperial Diet, opens, closes, and prorogues it, and dissolves the House of Representatives.

Article VIII. The Emperor, in consequence of an urgent necessity to maintain public safety or to avert public calamities, issues, when the Imperial Diet is not sitting, Imperial Ordinances in the place of law.

Such Imperial Ordinances are to be laid before the Imperial Diet at its next session, and when the Diet does not approve the said Ordinances, the Government shall declare them to be invalid for the future.

Article IX. The Emperor issues or causes to be issued, the Ordinances necessary for the carrying out of the laws, or for the maintenance of the public peace and order, and for the promotion of the welfare of the subjects. But no Ordinance shall in any way alter any of the existing laws.

Article X. The Emperor determines the organization of the different branches of the administration, and salaries of all civil and military officers, and appoints and dismisses the same. Exceptions especially provided for in the present Constitution or in other laws, shall be in accordance with the respective provisions (bearing thereon).

Article XI. The Emperor has the supreme command of the Army and Navy.

Article XII. The Emperor determines the organization and peace standing of the Army and Navy.

Article XIII. The Emperor declares war, makes peace, and concludes treaties.

Article XIV. The Emperor declares a state of siege. The conditions and effects of a state of siege shall be determined by law.

Appendix X

Article XV. The Emperor confers titles of nobility, rank, orders and other marks of honor.

Article XVI. The Emperor orders amnesty, pardon, commutation of punishments and rehabilitation.

Article XVII. A Regency shall be instituted in conformity with the provisions of the Imperial House Law.

The Regent shall exercise the powers appertaining to the Emperor in His name.

Chapter II: Rights and Duties of Subjects

Article XVIII. The conditions necessary for being a Japanese subject shall be determined by law.

Article XIX. Japanese subjects may, according to qualifications determined in laws or Ordinances, be appointed to civil or military or any other public offices equally.

Article XX. Japanese subjects are amenable to service in the Army or Navy, according to the provisions of law.

Article XXI. Japanese subjects are amenable to the duty of paying taxes, according to the provisions of law.

Article XXII. Japanese subjects shall have the liberty of abode and of changing the same within the limits of the law.

Article XXIII. No Japanese subject shall be arrested, detained, tried or punished, unless according to law.

Article XXIV. No Japanese subject shall be deprived of his right of being tried by the judges determined by law.

Article XXV. Except in the cases provided for in the law, the house of no Japanese subject shall be entered or searched without his consent.

Article XXVI. Except in the cases mentioned in the law, the secrecy of the letters of every Japanese subject shall remain inviolate.

Article XXVII. The right of property of every Japanese subject shall remain inviolate.

Measures necessary to be taken for the public benefit shall be provided for by law.

Article XXVIII. Japanese subjects shall, within limits not prejudicial to peace and order, and not antagonistic to their duties as subjects, enjoy freedom of religious belief.

Article XXIX. Japanese subjects shall, within the limits of law, enjoy the liberty of speech, writing, publication, public meetings and associations.

Article XXX. Japanese subjects may present petitions, by observing the proper forms of respect, and by complying with the rules specially provided for the same.

Article XXXI. The provisions contained in the present Chapter shall not affect the exercises of the powers appertaining to the Emperor, in times of war or in cases of a national emergency.

Appendix X

Article XXXII. Each and every one of the provisions contained in the preceding Articles of the present Chapter, that are not in conflict with the laws or the rules and discipline of the Army and Navy, shall apply to the officers and men of the Army and Navy.

Chapter III: The Imperial Diet

Article XXXIII. The Imperial Diet shall consist of two Houses, a House of Peers and a House of Representatives.

Article XXXIV. The House of Peers shall, in accordance with the Ordinance concerning the House of Peers, be composed of the members of the Imperial Family, of the orders of nobility, and of those who have been nominated thereto by the Emperor.

Article XXXV. The House of Representatives shall be composed of Members elected by the people, according to the provisions of the Law of Election.

Article XXXVI. No one can at one and the same time be a Member of both Houses.

Article XXXVII. Every law requires the consent of the Imperial Diet.

Article XXXVIII. Both Houses shall vote upon projects of law submitted to it by the Government, and may respectively initiate projects of law.

Article XXXIX. A Bill, which has been rejected by either the one or the other of the two Houses, shall not be brought in again during the same session.

Article XL. Both Houses can make representations to the Government, as to laws or upon any other subject. When, however, such representations are not accepted, they cannot be made a second time during the same session.

Article XLI. The Imperial Diet shall be convoked every year.

Article XLII. A session of the Imperial Diet shall last during three months. In case of necessity, the duration of a session may be prolonged by the Imperial Order.

Article XLIII. When urgent necessity arises, an extraordinary session may be convoked in addition to the ordinary one. The duration of an extraordinary session shall be determined by Imperial Order.

Article XLIV. The opening, closing, prolongation of session and prorogation of the Imperial Diet, shall be effected simultaneously for both Houses.

In case the House of Representatives has been ordered to dissolve, the House of Peers shall at the same time be prorogued.

Article XLV. When the House of Representatives has been ordered to dissolve, Members shall be caused by Imperial Order to be newly elected, and the new House shall be convoked within five months from the day of dissolution.

Appendix X

Article XLVI. No debate can be opened and no vote can be taken in either House of the Imperial Diet, unless not less than one-third of the whole number of Members thereof is present.

Article XLVII. Votes shall be taken in both Houses by absolute majority. In the case of a tie vote, the President shall have the casting vote.

Article XLVIII. The deliberations of both Houses shall be held in public. The deliberations may, however, upon demand of the Government or by resolution of the House, be held in secret sitting.

Article XLIX. Both Houses of the Imperial Diet may respectively present addresses to the Emperor.

Article L. Both Houses may receive petitions presented by subjects.

Article LI. Both Houses may enact, besides what is provided for in the present Constitution and in the Law of the Houses, rules necessary for the management of their internal affairs.

Article LII. No Member of either House shall be held responsible outside the respective Houses, for any opinion uttered or for any vote given in the House. When, however, a Member himself has given publicity to his opinions by public speech, by documents in print or in writing, or by any other similar means, he shall, in the matter, be amenable to the general law.

Article LIII. The Members of both Houses shall, during the session, be free from arrest, unless with the consent of the House, except in cases of flagrant delicts, or of offenses connected with a state of internal commotion or with a foreign trouble.

Article LIV. The Ministers of State and the Delegates of the Government may, at any time, take seats and speak in either House.

Chapter IV: The Ministers of State and the Privy Council

Article LV. The respective Ministers of State shall give their advice to the Emperor, and be responsible for it.

All Laws, Imperial Ordinances, and Imperial Rescripts of whatever kind, that relate to the affairs of the State, require the countersignature of a Minister of State.

Article LVI. The Privy Councillors shall, in accordance with the provisions for the organization of the Privy Council, deliberate upon important matters of State, when they have been consulted by the Emperor.

Chapter V: The Judicature

Article LVII. The Judicature shall be exercised by the Courts of Law, according to law, in the name of the Emperor.

The organization of the Courts of Law shall be determined by law.

Article LVIII. The judges shall be appointed from among those who possess proper qualifications according to law.

Appendix X

No judge shall be deprived of his position, unless by way of criminal sentence or disciplinary punishment.

Rules for disciplinary punishment shall be determined by law.

Article LIX. Trials and judgments of a Court shall be conducted publicly. When, however, there exists any fear that such publicity may be prejudicial to peace and order, or to the maintenance of public morality, the public trial may be suspended by provisions of law or by the decision of the Court of Law.

Article LX. All matters that fall within the competency of a special Court shall be specially provided for by law.

Article LXI. No suit at law, which relates to rights alleged to have been infringed by the illegal measures of the administrative authorities, and which shall come within the competency of the Court of Administrative Litigation specially established by law, shall be taken cognizance of by a Court of Law.

Chapter VI: Finance

Article LXII. The imposition of a new tax or the modification of the rates (of an existing one) shall be determined by law.

However, all such administrative fees or other revenue having the nature of compensation shall not fall within the category of the above clause.

The raising of national loans and the contracting of other liabilities to the charge of the National Treasury, except those that are provided in the Budget, shall require the consent of the Imperial Diet.

Article LXIII. The taxes levied at present shall, in so far as they are not remodelled by a new law, be collected according to the old system.

Article LXIV. The expenditure and revenue of the State require the consent of the Imperial Diet by means of an annual Budget.

Any and all expenditures overpassing the appropriations set forth in the Titles and Paragraphs of the Budget, or that are not provided for in the Budget, shall subsequently require the approbation of the Imperial Diet.

Article LXV. The Budget shall be first laid before the House of Representatives.

Article LXVI. The expenditures of the Imperial House shall be defrayed every year out of the National Treasury, according to the present fixed amount for the same, and shall not require the consent thereto of the Imperial Diet, except in case an increase thereof is found necessary.

Article LXVII. Those already fixed expenditures based by the Constitution upon the powers appertaining to the Emperor, and such expenditures as may have arisen by the effect of law, or that appertain to the legal obligations of the Government, shall be neither rejected nor reduced by the Imperial Diet, without the concurrence of the Government.

Appendix X

Article LXVIII. In order to meet special requirements, the Government may ask the consent of the Imperial Diet to a certain amount as a Continuing Expenditure Fund, for a previously fixed number of years.

Article LXIX. In order to supply deficiencies, which are unavoidable, in the Budget, and to meet requirements unprovided for in the same, a Reserve Fund shall be provided in the Budget.

Article LXX. When the Imperial Diet cannot be convoked, owing to the external or internal conditions of the country, in case of urgent need for the maintenance of public safety, the Government may take all necessary financial measures, by means of an Imperial Ordinance.

In the case mentioned in the preceding clause, the matter shall be submitted to the Imperial Diet at its next session, and its approbation shall be obtained thereto.

Article LXXI. When the Imperial Diet has not voted on the Budget, or when the Budget has not been brought into actual existence, the Government shall carry out the Budget of the preceding year.

Article LXXII. The final account of the expenditures and revenues of the State shall be verified and confirmed by the Board of Audit, and it shall be submitted by the Government to the Imperial Diet, together with the report of verification of the said Board.

The organization and competency of the Board of Audit shall be determined by law separately.

Chapter VII: Supplementary Rules

Article LXXIII. When it has become necessary in future to amend the provisions of the present Constitution, a project to the effect shall be submitted to the Imperial Diet by Imperial Order.

In the above case, neither House can open the debate, unless not less than two-thirds of the whole number of Members are present, and no amendment can be passed, unless a majority of not less than two-thirds of the Members present is obtained.

Article LXXIV. No modification of the Imperial House Law shall be required to be submitted to the deliberation of the Imperial Diet.

No provision of the present Constitution can be modified by the Imperial House Law.

Article LXXV. No modification can be introduced into the Constitution, or into the Imperial House Law, during the time of a Regency.

Article LXXVI. Existing legal enactments, such as laws, regulations, Ordinances, or by whatever names they may be called, shall, so far as they do not conflict with the present Constitution, continue in force.

All existing contracts or orders, that entail obligations upon the Government, and that are connected with expenditure, shall come within the scope of Article LXVII.

Index of Proper Names

Aoki Shuzo, 28, 32n., 70, 71
Arisugawa Taruhito, 5, 46, 51, 53n., 55, 58, 58n., 70
Baba Tatsui, 66
Clemenceau, Georges, 73
Enomoto Takeaki, 53n., 75n.
Eto Shimpei, 20, 27, 34
Fujita Toko, 2, 3
Fukuba Bisei, 46n.
Fukuchi Genichiro, 62, 63, 63n.
Fukuoka Kotei, 6, 8,17, 51n., 61n.
Fukuzawa Yukichi, 26, 33n., 57, 57n., 62
Furuzawa Uro, 67n.
Gneist, Rudolph, 58n., 70, 71, 72
Goto Shojiro, 6, 20, 26, 34, 37, 37n., 39, 66, 67n., 74n., 80, 81, 81n.
Hayashi Yuzo, 41n.
Hirata Tosuke, 69, 70n.
Hirosawa Sanetomi, 14, 74n.
Hosokawa Junjiro, 46n.
Inouye Kaori, 15, 20, 36n., 40, 49n., 50, 53n., 58n., 74n., 75n.
Inouye Kowashi, 58n., 59n., 61n., 63, 66, 69, 70n., 74, 77, 77n., 78, 78n., 79, 79n., 80
Inukai Tsuyoshi, 60n., 61n.
Itagaki Taisuke, 14, 17, 20, 26, 34, 35, 36, 36n., 37, 37n., 38, 39, 41, 61, 66, 67n., 74n., 76n., 80
Ito Hirobumi, 12, 14, 20, 26, 28, 33, 33n., 35, 38, 40, 40n., 47n., 48, 49, 49n., 50, 51n., 52, 53n., 54, 55, 55n., 56, 57, 57n., 58, 58n., 60, 61n., 63, 66, 69, 70, 70n., 71, 71n., 72, 72n., 73, 73n., 74, 74n., 75n., 76n., 77, 78, 78n., 79, 80, 80n., 81, 82, 82n, 83, 84n., 87n., 91, 92, 92n., 94n., 131
Ito Myoji, 69, 70, 70n., 71, 71n., 73, 74, 74n., 77, 78, 80
Iwakura Tomomi, 5, 9, 10, 10n., 15, 16, 17, 26, 27, 36, 36n., 40, 49, 49n., 52n., 53n., 55, 57, 58, 58n., 59, 66, 69, 70, 70n., 72, 72n., 73, 73n., 79n., 143
Iwasaki Yataro, 66
Jimmu, Emperor, 82, 104
Kaneko Kentaro, 74, 78, 78n., 80, 82n.
Kataoka Kenkichi, 41n., 42
Kato Hiroyuki, 26
Katsura Taro, 90n., 92n.

Kido Koin, 4, 5, 6, 9, 13, 14, 15, 15n., 16, 17, 20, 22n., 26 27, 28, 29, 30, 31, 32, 32n., 33, 34, 34n., 35, 36, 37, 38, 39, 40, 49n., 54, 62, 74n., 100, 133
Kitabatake Harufusa, 61n.
Kiyoura Keigo, 69
Komuro Nobuo, 67n.
Kono Hironaka, 42, 53n., 61
Kono Toshikama, 61n., 68
Kuroda Kiyotaka, 49n., 51, 53n., 56, 58n., 60n., 61n., 75n., 82, 94n.
Maejima Hisoka, 61n.
Maruyama Sakura, 62, 63, 63n.
Matsukata Masayoshi, 53n., 61n., 66, 75n., 90n.
Meiji, Emperor, 1, 46, 49, 53, 55, 56, 57, 58, 69, 70, 73, 82
Minobe Muneki, 84n.
Mizuno Torajiro, 62, 63, 63n.
Mori Arinori, 75n.
Mosse, Albert, 71n., 72, 72n., 78, 78n., 79, 79n.
Mutsu Munemitsu, 41n.
Nakashima Nobuyuki, 46n.
Nakayama Nobuyuki, 61
Nintoku, Emperor, 126
Numa Morikazu, 68
Oe Taku, 41n.
Oishi Masami, 66
Okamoto Takeo, 62, 63
Oki Takato, 49n., 50, 51, 52, 53n., 61n., 74n., 94n.
Okubo Toshimichi, 4, 5, 6, 9, 10, 10n., 13, 14, 15, 15n., 16, 17, 19n., 20, 22n., 26, 27, 33, 33n., 34, 34n., 35, 37, 37n., 38, 38n., 39, 40, 40n., 45, 47n., 49n., 55n., 74n., 111, 133
Okuma Shigenobu, 6, 20, 40, 40n., 49n., 52, 53, 53n., 54, 55, 55n., 56, 56n., 57, 57n., 58, 58n., 60, 60n., 61, 61n., 67n., 68, 74n., 75n., 76n., 136
Ono Azusa, 54n., 60n.
Ozaki Yukio, 60n., 61n., 68
Roessler, Hermann, 58n., 77, 77n., 78, 78n., 79n., 80
Saigo Takamori, 4, 5, 6, 16, 17, 20, 34, 36n., 38n., 39, 40, 41, 49n.
Saigo Tsugumichi, 53n., 58n., 60, 61n., 66, 75n.

157

Index

Saionji Kimmochi, 69, 70, 70n.
Sanjo Sanetomi, 5, 15, 16, 53n., 55, 56, 57, 58, 58n., 60, 70, 70n., 75 75n.
Sasaki Takayuki, 62
Shimazu Hisamitsu, 16, 37, 38, 38n.
Soejima Taneomi, 8, 16, 34
Spencer, Herbert, 73
Stein, Lorenz Von, 71, 71n., 72, 72n., 73
Suehiro Tetcho, 66
Sugida Seikei, 26
Taira Masakado, 113
Takeuchi Ko, 41n.
Tanaka Fujimaro, 53n., 69
Tani Kanjo, 75n.
Tani Tateki, 62
Tenchi, Emperor, 112

Terajima Munenori, 28, 40, 52n., 53n., 58n., 61n.
Todd, Alpheus, 47 47n.
Tokugawa Keiki, 4, 5
Veki Emori, 41n., 61
Uesugi Shinkichi, 84n.
Yamada Akiyoshi, 49n., 50, 52, 53n., 58n., 61n., 63, 66, 74n., 75.
Yamagata Aritomo, 15, 40, 46, 49n., 50, 53n., 58n., 75n., 76n., 81, 90n., 92n., 94n., 126
Yanagihara Sakimitsu, 46n.
Yano Fumio, 54n., 60., 61n.
Yoshida Masaharu, 41n.
Yoshida Shoin, 2, 3
Yoshi Tomozane, 47n.
Yuri Kimmasa, 12

JQ1611
.B4
1975

Beckmann

The making of the Meiji
  Constitution